SACRIFICE
AND SUFFERING

The Iraqi Turkmen's
Struggle to Survive

Edited by Kerkük Türkmenoðlu

DS 70.8
T85 S24

Printed in Canada

LIBRARY AND ARCHIVES CANADA CATALOGUING IN PUBLICATION

Sacrifice and suffering: the Iraqi Turkmen's struggle
to survive / edited by Kerkük Türkmenoglu

Includes index.
ISBN 1-895896-36-3

1.Turkmen--Iraq--History. 2.Iraq--History.
I. Türkmenoglu, Kerkük

DS70.8.T85S33 2006   956.7'00494364   C2006-902124-4

Printed and bound in Canada by Trico Group

Layout and Design by Esprit de Corps Books,
#204 - 1066 Somerset St. W., Ottawa, Ontario, Canada K1Y 4T3
Tel: (613) 725-5060 / Fax: (613) 725-1019
E-mail: espritdecorp@idirect.com
www.espritdecorps.ca

Table of Contents

PREFACE

Sacrifice and Suffering: The Iraqi Turkmen's Struggle to Survive is a unique addition to the reference material available on the modern Middle East, for several reasons. Although Iraq's third largest ethnic group, the Turkmen are often a forgotten entity in the overall political debate. Relatively unknown and relegated to virtual obscurity by the West, it is important to fully understand the Turkmen community and recognize their right to representation if Iraq is to successfully implement a peaceful path towards a future.

The purpose of this book is not to present an overview of the entire complex history and political divisions in northern Iraq. The intention is to provide the Turkmen peoples' perspective on the subjugation and oppression they suffered under successive tyrannical regimes as well as their hopes for a new identity in the post-Saddam era.

This book was produced with the co-operation of ITF representation offices from abroad.

ABOUT THE EDITOR

The *nom de plume* Kerkük Türkmenoðlu is used at the request of the editor for reasons of personal safety. With his family members still residing in northern Iraq, the editor fears that issues such as the Turkmen cause, which are considered sensitive to the Kurdish authorities, may incite retribution. The majority of the research and analysis was compiled with the assistance of the Iraqi Turkmen Front.

FOREWORDS
"WHAT'S A TURKMEN?"

July 26, 2005, Habur Gate, Northern Iraq – It had taken us hours to get through the clogged Turkey-Iraq border crossing and, were it not for some generous bribes and an intrepid driver, we would still be sweltering in the long lineup. While it is not my usual practice to jump a queue, in this instance a further delay would have jeopardized the scheduled rendezvous I had with American helicopters on the Iraqi side of the border.

When we finally reached the small U.S. military outpost at the expansive Habur Gate facility, the American soldiers there admitted they had no prior knowledge of our arrival, and certainly did not expect any helicopter flights. In true military "by the book" fashion, a staff sergeant condescendingly advised us that if we wished to visit U.S. troops in Telafer, we should try notifying the Pentagon first and then co-ordinate a travel plan through Kuwait.

The assembled soldiers lounging in the air conditioned cafeteria that hot day cordially offered us some cold pop and snacks, but it was evident from their amused glances that they believed the three of us foreign journalists must have been somewhat touched in the head by the excessive heat.

In this remote corner of Iraq, the U.S. garrison played no more than an observer's role as the actual border security was enforced by Kurdish warlord Massoud Barzani's peshmerga militiamen. The handful of American military police based at the customs house had made no attempt to intervene in either the issuing of visas or the collection of tax revenue. Two and a half years after the invasion to topple Saddam Hussein, the Kurdish provinces still operated as an autonomous region with no ties to the Baghdad central authorities. Not only did Barzani still maintain a private army, his Asaish (secret service) was also very much engaged in keeping their warlord in power.

Seated at a table pondering our next move, Sasha Uzunov, an Australian photo journalist, and Stefan Nikolawski, a Canadian documentary filmmaker, and I were approached in the U.S. cafeteria by a Kurdish Asaish agent. While the U.S. military personnel were prepared to dismiss our presence, the Asaish agent was intensely curious to learn more about our visit to Iraq. Having been detained and questioned by Barzani's secret service on previous trips into northern Iraq, I was amazed the Asaish would try to exert any kind of authority while inside an American military compound.

Not realizing the sensitivity of the situation, Uzunov engaged the Asaish agent in a friendly dialogue and advised him of our intention to report on the situation in Telafer – if and when the promised helicopters arrived. The very mention of the word Telafer started the Kurdish secret service agent to launch into a well-rehearsed diatribe about this little known city. When the Asaish operative tried to explain how Telafer was a "Kurdish" city being troubled by "Turkmen insurgents," I impolitely instructed him to "get the hell away from our table." Incensed at my tone, the Kurdish official grudgingly vacated his seat, moving a short distance away to where he could still monitor our conversation.

In order to enlighten my companions, I explained that during my previous 20 trips into Iraq I had grown weary of the constant Kurdish attempts to marginalize the Turkmen community with whom they share the northern provinces. I am one of a very few Westerners to ever visit the remote city of Telafer. On my second trip to this ancient city, in September 2004, I was seized and held hostage by the insurgents who now controlled the city. For five harrowing days me and a Turkish journalist, Zeynep Tugrul, were tortured, threatened with death, and at risk of being killed by the U.S. troops that were engaging our captors in fierce firefights. Since that time, Telafer has remained a hotbed of resistance to the U.S. occupation.

Such a rare inside look at the Iraqi insurgency had revealed a number of things to me – one of the most important being that a small chapter of Wahabbists known as Ansar al-Islam were active in Telafer. What made this discovery such a shock was that I had spent a great deal of time and effort researching the Iraqi Turkmen and in the post-U.S. invasion anarchy, I had made a dozen trips into northern Iraq but had not known the extremist group was operating in this remote region. I was fascinated with the complexity of the political and economic landscapes that seemed to be a lit powder keg poised to ignite a civil war and possibly fuel an even larger regional conflict.

At the centre of this brewing crisis was the disputed control of the Baba Gurgur oilfields outside of Kirkuk. In the immediate aftermath of Saddam's collapse, Kurdish peshmerga had rushed south from their autonomous provinces to lay claim to the oilriches of Kirkuk. With Baba Gurgur accounting for about 40 per cent of Iraq's oil exports, control of this asset would provide the Kurds with the economic means to declare an independent state. However, such a development runs counter to the political interests of Turkey, Iran, Syria and Armenia – four countries that border on northern Iraq and have substantial Kurdish minorities with strong separatist movements. Making matters even more complicated for the Kurds is the fact that Kirkuk has long been recognized in the history of Iraq as a Turkmen city.

Although no formal census has been taken since 1957, it is estimated that the Turkmen number as many as 3,000,000 – or up to 13 per cent of Iraq's 27 million population. However, in Kirkuk the indigenous Turkish-speaking Iraqi Turkmen represent more than 50 per cent of a population that also includes Kurds, Arabs, Chaldeans, Assyrians and Yazidi.

During his 30-year reign of terror, Saddam Hussein successfully marginalized the Turkmen through his Arabification policies. For their part, Kurdish warlords have taken every opportunity to keep the existence of this significant ethnic minority hidden from the Western media. As such, Turkmen are routinely listed among "others" in any analysis published concerning the demographics of Iraq. Those studying news reports from war-torn Iraq are familiar with the divisions of Shiite and Sunni Arabs and Kurds, but rarely is the term "Turkmen" ever seen in print.

To address this void, I wrote the book *Among the 'Others': Encounters with the Forgotten Turkmen of Iraq*. It provided some historical and political context on this community and, through the detailed account of my hostage experience, also provided insight into the complex networking of the local insurgent groups. In terms of international sales, *Among The 'Others'* was not a blockbuster, but it certainly has been widely circulated among the major stakeholders in Iraq – including members of the U.S. military.

One officer in particular, Colonel H.R. McMaster, took a keen interest in the book. McMaster was the commander of the 3rd Armoured Cavalry Regiment, one of the most combat-capable units in the U.S. Army. During the initial invasion of Iraq in 2003, 3ACR had played a pivotal role in crushing Saddam's forces. That was the role they were trained and equipped for, and the collapse of the Iraqi forces left them in the unfamiliar world of a burgeoning guerrilla war.

The U.S. troops had been promised they would be greeted as liberators and told they would return to America within six months. However, by the time 3ACR completed a full year tour of duty and had rotated home to Colorado Springs, they were advised that they would be redeployed back to Iraq within nine months. To prepare his men for their second tour, McMaster realized that a major shortcoming of his unit had been their inability to talk to the Iraqi people. In order to address this, the intrepid colonel ensured that each and every soldier in 3ACR mastered a basic proficiency in Arabic before returning to the Middle East.

By a twist of fate, the Pentagon assigned 3ACR to the Telafer sector. Very quickly the U.S. soldiers found out that their Arabic skills were useless when conversing with the Turkish-speaking locals. The officers of 3ACR were soon asking themselves, "What's a Turkmen?"

Soon after, Col. McMaster discovered my book *Among the 'Others'* and ordered his staff officers to contact me. Foregoing usual official Pentagon procedures, McMaster's officers called to offer me an "all expense paid trip to Telafer." In exchange, I was to provide the soldiers of 3ACR with a formal presentation about the Iraqi Turkmen and, in particular, the insurgents in Telafer. It was on the strength of this unusual request that I invited Sasha Uzunov and Stefan Nikolawski to join me in my rendezvous at the Habur Gate border post.

At 11:50 a.m., right on schedule, the distinct throbbing sound of approaching helicopters could be heard. The amused smiles of the GIs in the cafeteria quickly turned to awe as they rushed to the windows to watch the rare sight of a U.S. Army Blackhawk chopper land on a nearby soccer field as an Apache gunship menacingly swept across the rooftops. The Asaish agent was last seen making a flurry of phone calls as we hauled our gear aboard the Blackhawk and took off for Telafer.

The Turkmen were about to become a recognized piece of the post-war Iraqi puzzle.

Scott Taylor
Author and military analyst
Ottawa, Ontario, Canada
March 29, 2006

TURKMEN IN IRAQ – A HUNGARIAN VIEWPOINT

My first visit to Kirkuk was in September 2003. At that time, members of the Iraqi Turkmen Front had assembled to choose its new leader to replace the departing Sanan Ahmet Aga. The congress of the delegates had been watched over by American soldiers. I can still hear the Turkmen community's applause that greeted the American military commander who was present that day. It is quite possible that the American would have been welcomed with just as much enthusiasm only a few steps away from this location, at the Kurds' headquarters. The same man, however, would not have risked his life by making a public appearance in Fallujah or Tikrit. I thought to myself, then and there, that history, which forms right in front of our eyes, is quite complicated. Sometimes it isn't easy to know which is the oppressor and which is the defender.

However, there is only one Iraq – if we believe that the peoples living together picture their destiny and their future in one joint state. For a long time, similar to other Western journalists, I had only heard of the Turkmen. But looking back, I am proud to say that, unlike so many people in Europe, at least I had not mistaken them for the Turkmen living in the former Soviet Union. It is a special experience for a Hungarian journalist to meet Turkmen in Iraq. Probably not many people know that the Hungarians have not always lived in their European country.

Our ancestors arrived in Hungary from Asia in the 9th century. A century later they formed a Christian kingdom. A considerable number of historians and linguists believe that the old Hungarians were actually Turks from central Asia, and that we are genetically and linguistically closely related to Turks of the world. We Hungarians express the words "pocket," "aubergine," and "apple" the same way as our Turkmen friends in northern Iraq do. I was delighted to hear that, according to my Turkmen friends, my looks are also similar to theirs. That could be true, but I obviously still have to take lessons in Turkish – after all, one cannot speak to one's relatives in English. For someone who loves his home and cherishes the memory of his ancestors, it is always a great pleasure to be welcomed by friends.

Beyond my personal feelings for the Turkmen, I sympathize with them concerning certain political matters too. Hungarians know very well what it is like to be a minority. Because of certain historical events, one third of our nation was forced to live outside the borders of Hungary. Regarding the situation in northern Iraq, it has to be pointed out that all peoples of the world have the right to have autonomy. The Turkmen, descendants of the old Turks, should play an important part in the government of the new Iraq. This requires a firm strategy, clear political faith, and hard work.

Although Kirkuk and other towns in northern Iraq are full of blue-coloured houses, the Turkmen people have still not occupied their rightful place in the community of nations. It is necessary to work harder, a lot harder for the world to at least be aware of the existence of the Turkmen. As far as I know, the work has begun, but it would be an exaggeration to state that decision-makers of the European Union would be able to mark on a map the whereabouts of the Turkmen or, as a matter of fact, those of the Shia and Sunni Arabs or the Kurds. This situation needs to change because the future of the Turkmen is at risk. It is clear that Iraq is not the same country as it was under the regime of Saddam Hussein. I can remember this thought coming to my mind when my friend Scott Taylor and I had entered Iraq from Turkey in 2003.

We were greeted at the Kurd-controlled border of northern Iraq by a sign saying, "Welcome to Iraqi Kurdistan." The Turkmen should not have to fight the shadows of a dead family's empire, but instead should face the new challenges of the post-war era. The Turkmen must rely only on themselves, like they have so many times before in history. That is the destiny of all peoples with a small population. But we must not forget that "heart and free people can make great deeds," as a famous Hungarian poet once said. And only with strong heart can we gain freedom.

I trust that the Turkmen nation follows a path of wisdom, eventually becoming an appreciated member of the international community. This is in the interest of us all because benevolent people of the world hope to hear good news every day from Iraq, not tales of gunfire.

László Szentesi Zöldi
Journalist and foreign affairs adviser
Budapest, Hungary
April 6, 2006

In September 2003, Canadian journalist Scott Taylor (left) and Hungarian journalist László Szentesi Zöldi met with outgoing Iraqi Turkmen Front director Sanan Ahmet Aga.

WHO ARE THE TURKMEN?

The Turkmen are originally from the ancient Oguz Turkic tribes of Central Asia that migrated to different parts of the world, particularly Iraq, Iran, Syria and Turkey. Historians believe the first Turkmen settled in Iraq, then the southern part of Mesopotamia, around 3500BC, where an ancient Sumerian civilization of Turkic tribes was located.

The Turkmen have played a great role in Iraq's history. Before the Islamic conquest in the early part of the seventh century, the Turkmen lived in densely populated settlements throughout Iraq. Badikli and Bankiya were the largest of these ancient communities. Located near the Euphrates River, they were administrated by Baslukhan, a prominent Turkmen leader.

Over the centuries, the Turkmen established many dynasties and states in Iraq. The Oguz tribes that converted to Islam became known as Turkmen. Having earned a great reputation as disciplined warriors, 2,000 Turkmen archers were recruited into the army of Ubaydullah Bin Ziyad in the mid-seventh century in Basra in southern Iraq during the Ummayids (Ummawiyeen) era (AD 661-750). Hajjaj

Bin Yousuf Al Thakafi, another Ummayids commander, had settled 25,000 Turkmen warriors in Badra in eastern Iraq to defend the borders of the country. The Turkmen also had a great role in Iraq's military during the Abbasid era (AD 750-1258). Thousands of Turkmen soldiers settled in the city of Samarra, which was built for the troops and their families.

The largest number of Turkmen to move into Iraq occurred when the Seljuk army under the command of Sultan Tugrul Bey entered Baghdad in 1055. Another important age of migration occurred during the Ottoman Empire, which began with the reign of Suleiman the Magnificent and continued for more than four centuries.

TURKMEN DYNASTIES AND STATES IN IRAQ

- ❖ The Seljuk Empire (1055-1258)
- ❖ The Atabeg dynasty in Mosul (1127-1262)
- ❖ The Atabeg dynasty in Erbil (1144-1233)
- ❖ The Iwakiya or Kipchak dynasty in Kirkuk (1230-1296)
- ❖ The Ilhanlilar State (1258-1544)
- ❖ El-Celairi State (1339-1410)
- ❖ Karakoyunlu State (1411-1468)
- ❖ Ak Koyunlu State (1468-1508)
- ❖ The Safavid State (1508-1534)
- ❖ The Ottoman Empire (1534-1918)

LANGUAGE

The language spoken in different parts of Turkmen regions in Iraq is generally called the Turkmen language. It is very similar to the Turkish language with a slight difference in the dialect. The varying accents in the Turkmen regions (from Telafer to Mendeli) are indicative of the Turkmen migrations from Central Asia to Iraq that occurred over the centuries.

RELIGION

Before the introduction of Islam, the Turkmen practiced shamanism, which relates to the belief in spirits. Today, the majority of Turkmen inhabiting Iraq are Muslim, from both Sunni and Shiite sects. Those who converted to Christianity are called Christian Turkmen. They lived in the Citadel of Kirkuk, which was destroyed by the former regime of Saddam Hussein. Many Turkmen churches in Kirkuk are still open today for worship.

POPULATION AND CONTEMPORARY SETTLEMENT AREAS

The Turkmen are the third largest ethnic group after the Arabs and the Kurds in Iraq. Since 1921, only eight censuses have been conducted in Iraq. According to the 1957 census, at a time when Iraq's population was estimated at six million people, the Turkmen numbered 567,000. Considering a 3.2 per cent growth rate since 1957 and taking into account all available estimates of cities and townships where Turkmen live, the Turkmen population is estimated to be approximately three million people and they constitute around 13 to 16 per cent of the country's total population.

When the Turkmen people first immigrated to Mesopotamia in 3500BC, they settled primarily in the buffer zone between the Arabs and the Kurds in a very wide, expansive area that included six major provinces – Kirkuk, Mosul, Erbil, Diyalah, Salahaddin, and Baghdad. The Turkmen region (known as Turkmeneli) starts from the city of Telafer (enclosing more than 250 villages) in the northwest, to Mendeli and Aziziyah in the southeast of Iraq.

The region of Turkmeneli is one of the most strategically positioned areas in the world. Kirkuk, Mosul, and Hanakin sit on an ocean of oil, which is considered to be the second largest reservoir in the world after Saudi Arabia. Moreover, the Turkmeneli region has the most fertile soil in Iraq, with the Tigris River and many other branch rivers passing through the region. Thanks to its location, wealth in oil reserves and arable land, Kirkuk is the most desired province in all of Iraq.

ASSIMILATION AND MASSACRES

As will be described in more depth, the Turkmen people of Iraq have been undergoing decades of assimilation campaigns in their region and have been the targets of several wide-scale massacres since the 1920s. The first massacre occurred on May 4, 1924 and resulted in more than 100 Turkmen being killed and approximately 2,000 fleeing into exile.

In 1946, many Turkmen were killed and injured during the massacre of Gavurbagi. The three-day massacre of Kirkuk, which began on July 14, 1959, hit the Turkmen in the heart. Thirty-five Turkmen leaders and intellectuals were brutally massacred by the Kurds and more than 300 were wounded. During the 1991 uprising, hundreds of Turkmen were executed and thousands went missing.

That same year, Saddam Hussein's special forces executed more than 135 Turkmen in the township of Altun Kopru. Their bodies were later found in a mass grave in Dibis, near Kirkuk. Many Turkmen intellectuals were also killed during the invasion of the Iraqi army into the city of Erbil. Massoud Barzani, the leader of the Kurdistan Democratic Party (KDP), had co-operated with the Iraqi army in order to regain power from the Patriotic Union of Kurdistan (PUK), led by Jalal Talabani. The two Kurdish parties were fighting over control of northern Iraq and Kirkuk. Many Turkmen also lost their lives in Erbil during attacks in 1998 and again in 2000, when the KDP militia ransacked the Iraqi Turkmen Front's offices and buildings.

IRAQI TURKMEN FRONT (ITF)

The Iraqi Turkmen Front is a political organization that derives its power and legitimacy from the more than three million Turkmen living in the buffer zone between the Arabs and the Kurds. Established on April 24, 1995, the ITF is the only political organization in Iraq that strongly rejects an armed struggle and instead calls for territorial and political integrity. Throughout its history the ITF has always applied democratic rules in demanding the legitimate rights of the Turkmen people in Iraq while fully respecting the rights of all other Iraqi groups. The ITF also stands firmly against proposals aimed at disintegrating Iraq under different pretexts.

Since its inception, the organization has successfully conducted four general assemblies. The first assembly was held on October 7, 1997, and the second on November 22, 2000 in the city of Erbil. After struggling for more than 35 years under the tyrannical rule of the former Ba'athist regime, the ITF succeeded in conducting its third assembly in the Turkmen city of Kirkuk on September

13-15, 2003. Five hundred and fifty Turkmen delegates from six provinces – Mosul, Erbil, Kirkuk, Salahaddin, Baghdad, and Diyalah – participated to elect a president for the organization and a chairman of the Turkmen Council. Dr. Farouq Abdullah Abdurrahman was elected as the president of the ITF and Dr. Sadeddin Ergec (*pictured above*) became the chairman of the Turkmen Council. At the ITF's fourth assembly, which was held on April 22-24, 2005, Dr. Ergec was elected as the new president. On June 26, 2005, the Turkmen Council was reformed with 72 members and elected Yunus Bayraktar as chairman of the Turkmen Council.

The Iraqi Turkmen Front represents more than 90 per cent of the Turkmen in Iraq and has become an umbrella organization representing several Turkmen parties and organizations. The following parties and organizations have accepted the ITF for the legitimate representation of the Turkmen in Iraq:

- ❖ Iraqi National Turkmen Party – Iraq
- ❖ Turkmen Independents Movement – Iraq
- ❖ Iraqi Turkmen Islamic Movement – Iraq
- ❖ Turkmeneli Foundation for Cooperation and Culture – Turkey
- ❖ Turkmen Justice Party – Iraq
- ❖ Association for Turkmen Brotherhood – Iraq
- ❖ National Union of Turkmeneli – Iraq
- ❖ Turkmeneli Association of Intellectuals – Turkey
- ❖ Turkmen associations and human rights groups in the United Kingdom, Sweden, Holland, France, U.S.A., Australia, Canada, Turkey, Finland, Denmark, Norway, Belgium, Italy, Germany, Switzerland and Austria.

The Iraqi Turkmen Front has truly become an international organization, with offices in London, Washington, Berlin, Ankara and Syria as well as more than 100 offices across Iraq. The emblem of the ITF is a white crescent on a sky blue background with six white stars symbolizing the six states established by the Turkmen in Iraq.

IRAQ, A LAND OF CHANGE: 1914-1958

Before the First World War, Mesopotamia was divided into three major provinces – Mosul (Vilayet), Baghdad and Basra – and was under Ottoman rule. In 1914, Britain launched an offensive into Turk-occupied Mesopotamia in order to protect its interests in neighbouring Iran. In 1918, the country came under British occupation after the Ottoman army retreated to the province of Mosul, which it still controlled until Turkey's post-war collapse in 1919. Following years of unrest, the Kingdom of Iraq was established in 1921 with the exiled King Faisal the First being recalled from Lebanon and crowned king of the new State of Iraq. A treaty of alliance was established and the kingdom became a British protectorate.

After the First World War, the Turkmen people of Iraq experienced significant political and social distress. Following an agreement signed by Turkey, Iraq and Britain on June 5, 1926 in Ankara, the country of Iraq was redrawn. As a result, the state of Mosul – including the cities of Kirkuk, Erbil, Sulaimaniyah and Mosul proper – were left to Iraqi soil.

The ensuing new political and geographical structures served to isolate the Turkmen and they were condemned to oblivion when their rights as an ethnic group in Iraq were eroded. They were excluded from the political arena and became segregated in an occupied land. Although the Turkmen had shown no enmity against the new government of Iraq, they suffered horrific experiences. Many community leaders and intellectuals were arrested and thousands were exiled as they were seen as remnants of the Ottoman Empire.

Without the support and protection of the ruling government, the Turkmen, a pacific people, were left to their faith. In hindsight, their inability to demand political and social equality at this early stage in the development of the new state of Iraq was an unforgettable mistake, one for which they would continue to suffer from into the 21st century.

THE MASSACRE OF MAY 4, 1924

In 1924, Nestorian militias or levies (missionary soldiers that followed the early Christian doctrine of the ancient Churches of the Middle East) were sent to Kirkuk, where they moved into the existing army barracks inside the city. The Nestorian soldiers had started intimidating the Turkmen citizens to create unrest in the city. Although complaints were made to the British army commander in Kirkuk regarding the intimidations, no action was taken.

According to eyewitness accounts, the levies besieged the city of Kirkuk. On May 4, 1924, while the Turkmen were preparing to celebrate the first day of the Holly (Eid of Adha), Nestorian levies entered the Grand Bazaar and instigated an attack. In one instance, a Nestorian soldier who refused to pay for his merchandise attacked a Turkmen shopkeeper. The shopkeeper tried to defend himself but was killed by snipers stationed on the roof of Toma's House in the Citadel of Kirkuk facing the Grand Bazaar.

At that moment, thousands of Nestorians entered the bazaar and started shooting at the Turkmen civilians, randomly killing many, including women and children. Turkmen shops were completely destroyed after being looted and the Grand Bazaar was set on fire. The Nestorian soldiers tried to attack Turkmen women in the Women Public Bathhouse at the entrance of the Kirkuk Citadel, but faced a strong resistance by the men who defended their honour. The Turkmen in Kirkuk tried to protect themselves, while British aircraft dropped pamphlets written in the Turkish language asking people to remain calm and informing them that a curfew would be imposed on the city. The massacre started at the Eve of Eid and ended the following evening. More than 100 Turkmen were killed, including the sheikh's family.

Saki Ali Sadullah was among the Turkmen martyrs who defended the Women Public Bathhouse. He was killed when snipers

Toma's House in the destroyed Citadel of Kirkuk.

stationed on Toma's roof shot him. For his kindness and generosity, the Ottoman sultan's representative in Kirkuk gave his Grandfather Sadullah the name of Keshkuli. Keshkuli had helped the needy people for one month in the difficult days following the massacre. Saki Ali Sadullah was 23 years old and had three sons and one daughter (Hamid, Abdullah, Majid, and Meryem). He was buried at Sheik Jemil Cemetery. Another Turkmen martyr, Shishchi Mahmut, was found dead in his store; he had choked on tobacco leaves that had been stuffed down his throat.

Soon after the massacre, Turkmen intellectuals and teachers were exiled to the southern cities of Nasiriyyah and Al Basrah as punishment. Despite a government decision to compensate the aggrieved families, only a few Turkmen families actually benefited. Moreover, high-level government jobs were only given to non-Turkmen in the city of Kirkuk, which further raised tensions.

MASSACRE OF GAVURBAGI, JULY 12, 1946

Numerous incidents took place between 1930 and 1946, much to the detriment of the Turkmen. The government of Yasin Al Hashimi prohibited education in the Turkmen language and Turkmen people were arrested upon demanding their rights. As well, Turkmen employees of the Iraqi Petroleum Company (IPC) were laid off without benefits.

On July 12, 1946 an estimated 5,000 protestors demonstrated in front of the IPC office demanding their right to work. The Iraqi police opened fire on the crowd without any warning. Many Turkmen were killed and several arrested. A few days later, the government assembled a committee to investigate the situation and issued an order to allow the expelled labourers back to work. However, no investigation was carried out against the police officers involved in the massacre and only a few Turkmen were allowed to return to their jobs. A prominent Turkmen, Hayrullah Efindi, and two of his sons were arrested, badly tortured and pronounced dead shortly after.

A NEW ERA FOR IRAQ

Until the early 1950s, the Turkmen and Kurds had lived together in Iraq in peace and harmony. The Turkmen people have no enmity toward the Kurds or other ethnic groups inhabiting Iraq, such as the Arabs, Assyrians and Armenians. In fact, intermarriages relate many Turkmen and Kurdish families, which helped to strengthen the relationship between the two groups.

Kirkuk, the largest Turkmen city in northern Iraq, is very important to the Turkmen people as they have resided in this area for centuries and have a very strong historical connection to the region. Kirkuk is the most prosperous city in the region because of its strategic location, arable land, and its richness in natural resources – the city is floating over an ocean of oil. In fact, the huge oil reservoir that lies beneath the city has become Iraq's main source of income. Kirkuk is also considered the country's trade and business centre, facilitating a better life and employment opportunities for its citizens.

In the past 50 years, Kirkuk has become more diversified as changing economic conditions and poor living conditions in other areas have drawn people to this flourishing region. Well-established businesses and the openness of the Turkmen in accepting Kurdish settlement in the Turkmen localities of Shorija and Imam Kasim in the mid-20th century helped to create cohesion between the two groups. However, growing political instability and conflict between warring

Kurdish parties in northern Iraq along with poor living conditions forced many Kurds to migrate. The Kurdish immigration to Kirkuk occurred in various stages, with the first migration beginning in the early 1940s and the second in the late 1950s. With the Kurdish population in Kirkuk rapidly increasing, some of the traditional Turkmen areas soon became completely inhabited by Kurds. Upon considering the situation, the Turkmen sought out a solution to stem the Kurdish flow.

Realizing the importance of having their voice heard, the Turkmen established associations and organizations in Kirkuk. This distressed Kurdish nationalists and the Iraqi Communist Party, which already had a local committee in Kirkuk. The Turkmen were strongly opposed to the communist ideology, while the Kurds embraced it. In August 1956, Kurdish writer Najat Hadim Sujjade published an article in one of the Arabic newspapers in Baghdad that accused the Turkmen of being chauvinists. This initiated an argument between the two nations.

The student union was totally controlled by the Iraqi Communist Party and it intended to bring Turkmen students to its cause by establishing the "Turkmen Democratic Student Union" at the University of Baghdad. The union circulated some pro-communist pamphlets and called on Turkmen students to enroll, but the motivation was strongly condemned and a lack of interest in joining the union forced the Communist Party to terminate the organization. The second attempt to persuade the Turkmen to join the Communist Party was by contacting Turkmen intellectuals Abdulezel Abdulhadi Mufti and Dr. Nizameddin Arif. Unfortunately for the Communists, both had strongly rejected the idea after consulting their colleagues in Kirkuk.

The dispute between the Iraqi Communist Party and the nationalists was unmanageable; yet, the Communists occupied most of the important positions in Iraq, and organizations such as the student union, the media, the workers union, and the Ministry of Education. They also established small military groups called Public Resistance Armies. The majority of the Kurds had joined the Iraqi Communist

Party and used the party's authority for their benefit. As such, Kurds were appointed to positions in important offices in Kirkuk and, as such, control of the region soon was in their hands. They used the Communist Party as an umbrella to hide underneath and to achieve their goals as Kurdish nationalists. They celebrated the transition of power by gathering in large groups and shouting anti-Turkmen slogans, which intensified the tension between the two sides and eventually required the involvement of the Iraqi army.

In an attempt to ease the tension in a peaceful manner, General Nazim Tabakchali, the commander of the Second Army Division, ordered both sides to establish the National Solidarity Committee. Representatives from both cultures agreed to begin the negotiations. The Kurds sent lawyers Mukarram Al Talabani, Hussein Al Barzanji, and Omer Mustafa, as well as retired Colonel Abdulkadir Al Barzanji. The Turkmen meanwhile were represented by lawyers Mohammed Haji Hussein and Tahsin Rafet, retired Colonel Ata Hayrulla, and pharmacist Majeed Hassan. Although minor incidents occurred during this period, they were controlled by direct army involvement.

GENERAL ABDUL KARIM KASSEM TAKES CONTROL

This tense situation continued until July 14, 1958, when Iraqi General Abdul Karim Kassem staged a successful military coup, sending the country into another period of transition. Kassem quickly assumed control of the country and the last of the British troops soon withdrew from Iraq.

Before long, Baghdad radio was broadcasting news of the military coup d'état mounted by General Abdul Karim Kassem and his second-in-command, Colonel Abdul Salam Arif, both from the "Free Officers Movement." The royal regime had been overthrown and King Faisal the Second, the Regent, Prime Minister Nuri Saed and other monarchy politicians were killed. The Revolutionary Council headed by Gen. Abdul Karim Kassem publicly announced that the monarchy had been replaced by a new republic.

The Turkmen were astonished when the new leaders addressed

the nation and stated that Arabs, Kurds and Turkmen constituted the population of Iraq. They also stated the Turkmen were the third largest segment of the population and that they had been deprived of basic human rights during Nuri Saed's tyranny (Saed had not hidden his prejudice of the Turkmen people).

This affirmation of their status as an important nation of Iraq had encouraged the Turkmen to embrace the new Republican regime. They believed they would obtain their legitimate rights in different aspects and that Turkmen candidates would be allowed to participate in the Iraqi parliament. Thinking of social justice, political freedom and democracy, hundreds of congratulation letters were sent to the Republican government in Baghdad.

Two weeks after the coup, Turkmen convoys from Kirkuk, Erbil, Mosul, Telafer, Kifri, and other Turkmen suburbs participated in the celebrations, despite the imposed curfew. More than 100 cars and buses gathered in the Baghdad Al Jadida (New Baghdad) district waiting for Turkmen leader Ata Hayrullah to lead the convoy. The Turkmen procession approached the gathering point in front of the University of Baghdad's engineering department then headed towards the defence ministry where Gen. Kassem had made a speech earlier promising ethnic rights for all Iraqi segments, including the Turkmen.

On September 23, 1958 a group of Turkmen intellectuals began *Al Bashir*, a journal published in Arabic and Turkmen languages. As well, the first daily Turkmen radio show began in early February 1959. Broadcast from Baghdad, the show was extended from a half hour to four hours. However, in March 1959, after only 26 issues were published, *Al Bashir* was stopped by orders from the military. On March 18, 1959, Ata Terzibashi, a well-known lawyer and the editor of *Al Bashir*, was arrested. At the same time, famous Turkmen leaders Mehmet Izzet Hattat, one of the directors of the journal, and Habib Hurmuzlu, the owner of *Al Bashir*, were arrested and exiled to Nasiriyyah, approximately 500 kilometres south of Kirkuk**.**

However, after only three months, ideological differences between coup leaders General Abdul Karim Kassem and his second-in-command Colonel Abdul Salam Arif grew and their union collapsed when the latter was arrested. Arif, an Arab nationalist and a strong supporter of former Egyptian president Jamal Abdul Naser, had supported the idea of forming the United Arab Republic and uniting with Egypt.

When Gen. Kassem formed the first cabinet, four of the 12 ministers were from the Iraqi Communist Party. Kamil Kazanchi, who had spent many years studying in Moscow, was appointed to the Society Resistance Army founded by Kassem. Approximately 1,000 people were arrested with the intervention of military units in Baghdad. Gen. Kassem had contacted the Soviet Union and the Iraqi army was furnished with Russian weapons. Approximately 1,000 doctors, 1,053 agriculture engineers, 142 petrol technicians and hundreds of military experts were also brought from the U.S.S.R.

However, supporters of deposed Colonel Abdul Salam Arif could not be kept silent. The first revolt against the Communist Party came from Lieutenant-Colonel Abdulwahab Al Shawwaf in Mosul in March 1959, but it was suppressed by the Communists and hundreds lost their lives. A few days later, General Nazim Tabakchali, the commander of the Second Army Division in Kirkuk and a Turkmen partisan, was arrested and executed.

During this period, the political instability in northern Iraq intensified as Kurdish separatists, who held the balance of the political power in the region, began planning for their own sovereignty and changing the identity of the Turkmen city of Kirkuk. Kurdish separatists planned to slaughter the Turkmen population then declare Kirkuk the capital of a newly-created Kurdistan. But the Kurds were forgetting their history and the support the Turkmen extended them during their earlier ordeals.

Maruf Al Barzanji, a Kurdish Communist leader who had spent most of his life among the Turkmen in Kirkuk, was one of those involved in the massacre. He studied law at the University of Baghdad and was involved in the communist movement after spending many years in Moscow. As a result, he became an active member in the Iraqi Communist Party and held the position of secretary in the Ansar Al Salam Communist group in Kirkuk. Although his wife was actually a Turkmen, this did not diminish his hatred of the Turkmen people. He and his brother Hussein, along with other militant Kurds, planned and waited for an opportunity to come.

In the early 1940s, Mulla Mustafa Al Barazani, the founder of the Kurdistan Democratic Party and a man determined to establish a separate Kurdish state, fled to the Soviet Union. After 11 years in Moscow, he was promoted to the rank of general in the Russian army. When the declaration of a general amnesty was given by Gen. Kassem, Al Barazani and many other political dissidents returned to Iraq. In October 1958, Gen. Kassem also ordered the release of all political prisoners. Al Barazani was given a very enthusiastic welcome and spent two days in one of the governmental palaces in Baghdad. Immediately upon his return, he discussed the issue of Kurdish autonomy in northern Iraq with Gen. Kassem and of adding Kirkuk to their map.

After visiting fellow separatists in Sulaimaniyah, Mullah Mustafa Al Barazani travelled to Kirkuk where he was welcomed in the officers' guesthouse. On October 22, 1958, Al Barazani spoke to a large crowd of Kurds that had come from near and far to hear their leader speak. But at 5:00 p.m., after Al Barazani had left for Baghdad, the Kurdish uprising began in Kirkuk. Reinforced by others who had come from outside the city, the Kurds began to chant anti-Turkmen slogans: "Kirkuk is a Kurdish city! Death for the Turkmen! Kirkuk is the heart of Kurdistan! Turkmen get out of our Kurdish city! Long live

Mullah Mustafa Al Barazani (front left) and Saddam Hussein (front centre) in the 1970s. The Ba'ath Party supported Al Barazani's Kurdish party.

Barazani! We are in Kurdistan! Kirkuk is part of Kurdistan!"

A group of armed Kurdish separatists had stopped by the Yildiz Café and began chanting provocative anti-Turkmen slogans. Another group was calling for the Turkmen to evacuate the city. Some Turkmen tried to get involved but were prevented by their leaders. Soon, things got out of control and some Turkmen were attacked and some of their stores and businesses were destroyed. Many of the Kurdish soldiers serving in the Fourth Army Brigade joined the Public Resistance Army and took part in the riot. Thanks to the quick reaction of General Nazim Tabakchali, a general massacre against the Turkmen was averted. Tabakchali promptly ordered the arrest of the aggressors and requested that the National Solidarity Committee come to Kirkuk to relieve the tension.

The behaviour of the Kurdish people had astonished the Turkmen. In another instance, a large group of Kurds had gathered in front of the Bayat Turkmen café (Turkmen leaders often met at cafés to discuss matters; and as a result, many were targetted during attacks). Although the Turkmen tried to prevent a clash and resolve the situation peacefully, the separatist communist Kurds struck.

Members of the KDP alleged that a bomb was found under the vehicle of their leader and that the Turkmen were attempting to assassinate Mulla Mustafa Al Barazani. They also claimed that a Kurdish soldier had dismantled the bomb. However, the army bomb squad in Kirkuk investigated the event and disproved the allegations when they found no evidence that a bomb had even existed. It is believed that by making these false allegations, the KDP was hoping to gain the sympathy of the Kurdish population in Kirkuk whom they wanted to turn against the Turkmen.

A deteriorating situation made the Kirkuk army garrison commander, Major Hidayet Arslan, step in and attempt to prevent the carnage. Three days later, on October 25, 1958, Major Arslan was pronounced dead at the army hospital in Kirkuk.

WHO WAS MAJOR HIDAYET MOHAMMED ARSLAN?
Hidayet Mohammed Arslan was born in 1910 in the Turkmen vil-

lage of Turkalan, located 10 kilometres south of Kirkuk. He originated from a large Turkmen tribe in the village and completed high school in Kirkuk. He joined the army college in Baghdad and graduated as an officer in the Iraqi army where he participated in several events and took many army courses until 1936.

During the Second World War, Arslan was transferred to the Third Border Guard Regiment. He was promoted in 1947 to the position of deputy commander of the Second Garrison Division and was given a commanding position in 1948 in Palestine. After occupying several positions, he became the commander of the Second Garrison Regiment of Kirkuk on June 15, 1957. Major Hidayet Mohammed Arslan (*pictured above*) was married, had six sons and three daughters, and was seen as a leader of the Turkmen and a patriot who loved both his country and his people. (One of his sons, Dr. Muzaffer Arslan, a general practitioner, would serve as president of the Turkmen National Party and as a Turkmen advisor to Iraqi president Jalal Talabani, a Kurd, in 2005.)

When Kurdish separatists gathered in front of the Turkmen Al Majidiyyah Café on October 22, 1959 to welcome the return of Mullah Mustafa Al Barazani, they held banners and placards and shouted anti-Turkmen slogans. The local Kurds had invited Kurdish villagers from outside the city to meet their leader with false promises that the Iraqi Communist Party would distribute farm equipment to those who participated in the rally. The Communist Party appears to have

These photographs were taken at Major Hidayet Arslan's funeral.

played a hand in the brainwashing of the naïve Kurdish farmers. Party members visited poor Kurdish villages and met others in mosques promising them a separate Kurdish state and subsidies, such as land, farm animals, and agricultural tools and equipment. They were empty promises, and the poor Kurdish farmers were easily deceived.

Major Arslan had been aware that the situation between the Kurds and the Turkmen was growing more tense, but he had always tried to resolve issues peacefully before they got out of hand. This was the case during the rally of October 22, 1958. However, three days later, he was dead.

Although the actual cause of death remains unknown, several theories arose. At the time many believed he was targeted by Kurdish separatists for his actions during the riot, others thought he had been poisoned while some supposed he had been wounded. A well-known and beloved leader, all Turkmen schools and businesses were closed in Kirkuk for the funeral. During the funeral procession on October 26, 1958, a clash almost erupted between more than 60,000 Turkmen and Kurds, but Colonel Ata Hayrullah managed to ease the tension and the ceremony ended peacefully.

WHO WAS GENERAL NAZIM TABAKCHALI?

On December 26, 1958, during a short absence by General Nazim Tabakchali, commander of the Second Army Division, the Kurds sent a convoy to meet with Gen. Abdul Karim Kassem in Baghdad to discuss some national security issues. During this meeting they accused the Turkmen of planning an uprising and plotting a coup against the government. They also alleged that the Turkmen were heavily armed and storing military equipment in three different villages around Kirkuk. The names and addresses of 27 Turkmen accused of these charges were passed to the Iraqi government officials. Upon hearing these claims, Kassem consulted his interior minister, Ahmet Mohammed Yahya, who told him the allegations were false. As well, Yahya explained to Gen. Kassem that the only armed people in Kirkuk were the Kurds.

This event in particular was detailed by Gen. Tabakchali at his trial. (He was brought up on charges relating to Lt.-Col. Abdulwahab Al Shawwaf's rebellion in March 1959 in Mosul.) In his defence, Tabakchali stated that, "The plan to search the Turkmen houses was prepared ahead [of time] and [was] well-planned and influenced by the Kurds. On December 26, 1958 a group of Kurds met with the prime minister to inform him that the Turkmen have been armed and that they have stored weapons in 27 Turkmen houses and three villages."

Instructions had been issued from Baghdad to investigate the situation. According to military telegram number 393 issued by the General Military Command on December 26, 1958, a search team consisting of more than 40 army personnel was sent to investigate the claims. The first of the houses searched belonged to Ibrahim Al Nafitchi, Colonel Ata Hayrullah, Colonel Ihsan Hayrullah and Colonel Shilemon Khoshaba, an Assyrian. Kitchen knives from Al Nafitchi and licensed guns belonging to Shilemon, Ata and Ihsan along with hunting guns and some bullets belonging to Kassem Beg Nafitchi were confiscated. Many Turkmen dwellings were ransacked and destroyed by the Public Resistance Army, which carried out the search. This action served to further deteriorate the situation in Kirkuk.

On January 13, 1959 the Public Resistance Army, augmented by a group of Kurds, invaded the July 14 Café on Al Hamra Street –named after the date of General Kassem's military coup that brought him to power – and many people from both sides were injured. The violence continued and a group of Kurds attacked Turkmen neighborhoods and killed many civilians, but after the National Solidarity Committee became involved the intensity of the attacks diminished.

Although the Iraqi Communist Party had succeeded in receiving the support of General Abdul Karim Kassem, in early 1959 the party was defeated in the local elections in Kirkuk. After an overwhelming victory in the elections, the Turkmen now occupied the top positions. But it did not take long for President Kassem's government to issue a directive that saw the removal of the Turkmen from office and the balance of power shifted once again as the elected Turkmen were replaced by Kassem Communist Party loyalists, the majority of whom were Kurds. Most of the governmental and administrative jobs were granted to Communist Party members, while many Turkmen were left unemployed.

Davud Al Janabi, a communist extremist, was appointed as high commander of the Second Army Division in Kirkuk. Maruf Al Barzanji, an unelected Kurd, was appointed as mayor of Kirkuk. Another communist extremist named Ojeen was appointed as the commander of the Public Resistance Army. Orders were then issued from Baghdad to have Turkmen intellectuals and businessmen arrested.

On March 1, 1959, during a morning gathering, Lebibe Ahmet Elreyyis, the principal of the female teachers' school in Kirkuk, spoke out against the Turkmen in general. Her incendiary lecture led to a clash between the Turkmen students and the principal. Before long the news spread all over Kirkuk. Turkmen parents and their children gathered in front of the school demanding to meet with Principal Ahmet Elreyyis and ask her to explain her behaviour. When she refused to meet with them, the Turkmen smashed the school windows in anger and frustration. Communist security forces were called in to escort Ahmet Elreyyis out of the school.

The dispute continued until the Second Army commander, Lieutenant-Colonel Abdulwahab Al Shawwaf, rebelled against the Communists in Mosul on March 8, 1959. Lt.-Col. Al Shawwaf was an Arab nationalist with an outstanding reputation in the army. Orders had been given to the garrison to bomb Mosul from the air and two days later the Communists took control of the city. The riot lasted four days and the Turkmen resistance was brutally suppressed. Many people were executed and some were sentenced to life imprisonment. Lt.-Col. Al Shawwaf was taken to the hospital after being wounded, and was stabbed to death shortly after.

This was an exceptional opportunity for the Communists and the Kurds to indict the commander of the Second Army Division, General Nazim Tabakchali. Although an Arab nationalist, he was well versed in politics and sympathized with the Turkmen position. He was appointed July 16, 1958 as commander of the Second Army Division based in Kirkuk. He admired the Turkmen and had an excellent relationship with them. In his memoirs, which were published many years after his death, Tabakchali revealed several facts about the ethnic composition of Kirkuk and why he, in particular, had been appointed to a position in Kirkuk.

Tabakchali had been aware of Kurdish plans to take over the city and alter the Turkmen identity of Kirkuk. During clashes between the Kurds and Turkmen, Tabakchali always advised the Turkmen not to retaliate and to remain calm. He had always tried to establish conditions of peace and harmony among the different ethnic groups that lived in the area. In his memoirs, he revealed some of the secret reports Gen. Kassem had sent him by means of military intelligence regarding the tension and the incidents that took place in Kirkuk. In a report dated September 9, 1958, Tabakchali had warned Kassem:

"Kirkuk citizens are not Kurds and it is not a Kurdish city, but Kurds are trying to dominate Kirkuk and to control oil resources, which is considered as national revenue of the Republic of Iraq. Creating the Centre of the Kurdistan Education Directorate in Kirkuk and [appointing a Kurd as director] is definitely inappropriate. The education director in Kirkuk must be a neutral and impartial person. … Please pay attention to the reports that I have previously sent to you; the Kurds will include Kirkuk in Kurdistan even if the majority of the citizens in Kirkuk are Turkmen."

Tabakchali also indicated that the Kurds were building villages around the city and encouraging the Kurds from the north to settle around the area of Kirkuk. He continuously passed this information on to Baghdad and urged officials to prevent these events, with the warning that doing nothing could have serious consequences.

Despite his best efforts to defend himself, General Nazim Tabakchali was found guilty for his role in Al Shawwaf's rebellion in Mosul and was sentenced to death. He was replaced by a Kurd, Colonel Asad Baban, and shortly thereafter Communist Davud Al Janabi was appointed as commander.

POLITICAL INSTABILITY IN KIRKUK

The situation in Kirkuk was changing rapidly and things were about

RIGHT: *Logo of the Iraqi Turkmen Front (ITF).*
BOTTOM: *The blue stripe in the map of Iraq indicates contemporary Turkmen settlement areas. The Turkmen first came to Iraq (then Mesopotamia) in 3500BC. The city of Kirkuk is located in the centre of the Turkmen zone.*

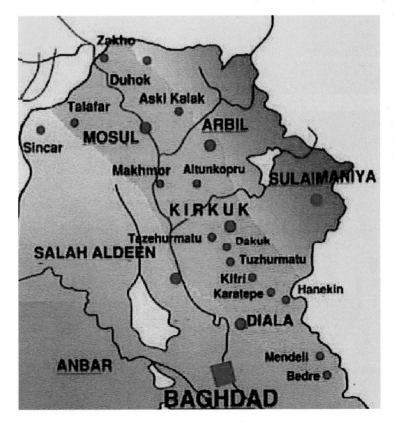

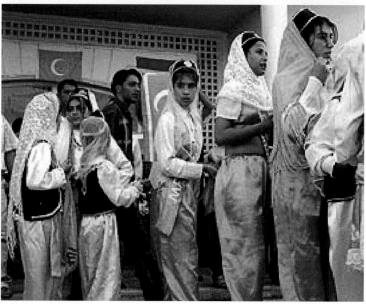

Examples of traditional Turkmen dress. The Turkmen folklore is very old and dates back thousands of years. The national dance performed by the Turkmen is called Halay. Halay means "many people" and the dance is performed in nearly every part of the Turkmen region known as Turkmeneli.

More examples of traditional Turkmen costumes, which are also worn by children on special holidays and occasions. The blue and white colors are representative of the Turkmen people, and are seen in their national flag and costumes.

*Two views of the northern city of Kirkuk, established centuries ago
by the Turkmen. The photograph above dates back to the 1960s,
while the other, with the Khasa Su River in the foreground, was taken
in the early 1980s. Kirkuk is the most prosperous city in the region
because of its strategic location, arable land, and its richness in natural
resources. The huge oil reservoir that lies beneath the city has become
Iraq's main source of income.*

The top photo shows the Citadel of Kirkuk before its destruction in the early 1980s. Below is the only part of Toma's house in the Citadel of Kirkuk that remains standing today. This structure is very important to the Turkmen people because it is from atop this vantage point that Nestorian snipers opened fire into the Grand Bazaar below (foreground), killing Turkmen as they prepared to celebrate Eid of Adha. This remaining section was saved to remember the Turkmen who lost their lives in the May 4, 1924 massacre.

Above, the ruins of a castle that dates back to the Crusades dominates the skyline of the ancient Turkmen village of Telafer, an area that is rarely visited by Westerners. Under successive regimes, especially the Ba'ath Party's system of tribal patronage and policies of Arabification, Turkmen settlements such as Telafer were impoverished through years of deliberate government neglect.

Two views of the headquarters for the Iraqi Turkmen Front in Kirkuk.

to erupt. Upon his appointment, Davud Al Janabi took the opportunity to attack the Turkmen media and community leaders. The *Kirkuk* newspaper, which was issued by city hall, and two other Turkmen papers, *Al Bashir* and *Al Afak,* were rescinded. Some of the papers' employees along with other Turkmen lawyers, physicians and activists were arrested and some were exiled. Al Janabi also issued a search warrant to look for weapons in Turkmen homes, but nothing incriminating was found. It is believed that this action was done in preparation for the massacre as a means of making sure the Turkmen were disarmed.

Following the search, the names of more than 100 Turkmen and nationalist Arab officers were given to Baghdad. They were then transferred to different cities and most of the top positions of authority were given to Kurds. Colonel Asad Baban was appointed deputy army commander, Colonel Mohammed Al Khafaji (an Arab communist) became commander of the Second Army Division, Colonel Abdurrahman Al Kazi (a Kurd) became commander of the Artillery Division, Captain Nezhet Al Kazzaz (a Kurd) was promoted to commander of Army Intelligence Service, Major Neshet Al Sunuwi (a Kurd) became garrison commander and Captain Fakhri Kareem (an Arab communist) was named as his deputy.

The Kurds had gained control of the city through the support of Davud Al Janabi, who started his position on March 14, 1959. He appointed Kurdish judges and hired some of his comrades and old friends for sensitive positions: Retired major Fatih Davoud Al Jabbari was in charge of political and civil affairs in Kirkuk; Maruf Al Barzanji, a communist Kurd and secretary of Ansar Al Salam, was appointed mayor of Kirkuk; Awni Yousuf from the Kurdish Democrats was appointed attorney general; Mahdi Hamid, also a communist Kurd, was named head of the National Resistance Army; Abdul-Jabbar Peruz Khan became head of the Democratic Youth.

As thousands more Kurds settled in Kirkuk, the uneasiness of the Turkmen increased as they realized their traditions and history were eroding and they were becoming an ethnic minority in their own city. After provocative pamphlets against the Turkmen were distributed in Kirkuk, they were sent to Baghdad for investigation but without reply. Land and building permissions were issued only to the Kurds. The Kurds soon outnumbered other groups in the districts of Shorija and Raheem Awa.

On March 22, 1959 the Communist Party Committee of Kirkuk announced that extremists were trying to create fear and hatred among the Arabs, Kurds and Turkmen and called on all people to be attentive and cautious. Consequently, many Turkmen were exiled and more than 3,000 were arrested under various allegations. Leaders of the National Turkmen Movement were also arrested; some were sentenced to prison terms and others exiled. After these major transformations, the Kurds now had the political, economical and decision-making power in the city of Kirkuk and were backed by the Iraqi Communist Party.

The sudden transfer of Gen. Davud Al Janabi and Mahdi Hamid in June 1959 displeased the Kurds since it was thought these individuals could help to cover crimes committed against the Turkmen. General Mahmut Abdulrazzak was put in command of the Second Army Division. Despite a Kurdish delegation's best efforts to have Al Janabi appointed for a second term, he was never reinstated.

MASSACRE OF JULY 14, 1959

To mark his assumption of power, the people of Iraq celebrated the government of Abdul Karim Kassem on every 14th of July. This date marked a new era within the Republic of Iraq and it was celebrated with much enthusiasm and jubilation by its people. But in 1959, this date would have a new meaning for the Turkmen.

The largest Turkmen gathering was in front of Aslan Yuvasi, a place in the Musalla region where celebrations were often held. Other ethnic groups had also come to celebrate the new government. The celebration began at 8:00 a.m., when the army troops marched in front of the Army Locale and continued until noon. Despite the scorching heat, the Turkmen had dressed in their colorful national costumes, sang and performed national dances. Carrying flowers, Turkmen women and children also participated in the celebration. Houses and governmental buildings were all decorated and the voices of children singing the national anthem and Turkmen songs could be heard from a distance.

At six o'clock, the evening celebrations began with a parade. Hundreds of Communist followers and activist groups such as The Forward Youth, Peace-Loving Revolutionist Teachers, and People Resistance Organization were ready to participate in the festivities. Meanwhile, a group of communist Kurds staged an armed political demonstration. Hundreds of Kurds had assembled mainly on Atlas, El-Awkaf and Al-Majidiyyah streets of Kirkuk, their number augmented by others brought up from different villages on false allegations that the Turkmen had committed genocide against them. When the Turkmen people started to march towards Atlas Street, they were met by a large group of Kurds who were shouting anti-Turkmen slogans such as: "Forward, Forward dear Karim, there is no Arab, no Islam," and began throwing stones and taking out ropes and weapons.

The explosion went off around 6:00 p.m. on July 14, 1959; it marked the start of the Turkmen massacre in Kirkuk. When the Turkmen realized what was going on, it was too late. Shots were fired at the Turkmen who had gathered in the Al Shabab, a large café on Atlas Street in Kirkuk. Osman Hidir, the owner of the café was

This photograph of Turkmen children was taken before the massacre.

heinously murdered and dragged behind a jeep on the streets. Many Turkmen lost their lives in the attack and others injured before the crowd dispersed. Militant Kurds began destroying and burning the Victory Arcs. The city of Kirkuk was cordoned off and the garrison commander imposed an immediate curfew for the Turkmen while the Kurds were allowed to move freely. Many of the Turkmen leaders' homes had been vandalized in the preceding weeks and their doors were marked with a red (X) sign.

The Fourth Army Battalion, which consisted mainly of Kurds and communists, had positioned their troops to prevent any communications that might be requested. The Citadel of Kirkuk was bombed following the announcement by Majid Hassan, a communist commander who issued the arrest warrant for Turkmen leader General Abdullah Abdurrahman.

Many houses and old Turkmen churches and mosques were destroyed and the streets of Kirkuk were stained with blood. The Kurdish separatists and the Public Resistance Army led by Ojeen had taken total control of Kirkuk. Many Turkmen were arrested and taken to army barracks; several were taken from their houses and brutally executed in front of the army barracks known as Kirkuk Kishlasi. Many Turkmen were viciously butchered, bayoneted and butted to

Victory Arcs on Atlas Street in Kirkuk before they were vandalized during the massacre of July 14, 1959.

death. Others were taken from their houses and dragged through the streets of Kirkuk and hanged from trees and electric posts. A number of intellectuals were tied to cars heading opposite directions. Iron bars were used to gouge out their eyes while they were still alive, others were dragged behind cars for many kilometers and several were buried alive.

The horrified pregnant had miscarriages and others were psychologically affected while their beloved were brutally killed in front of their eyes. A number of Turkmen children were killed in their cribs while mothers were forcibly taken into the army barracks. The prisons were all over-crowded and many schools were converted into prisons. The brutality continued and Turkmen shops, houses and trade centers were looted and set on fire by Kurdish pillagers. Fire trucks were stopped from putting out fires in different parts of the city. The Kurdish militias who occupied the hospitals prevented the treatment of wounded Turkmen.

Three days of violence passed slowly. Turkmen corpses were left to rot on the streets in the hot July sun. The army then received orders to bomb the Citadel of Kirkuk and to destroy Turkmen houses. Artillery was used to destroy the Atlas and Alameyin cinemas. The two brothers that owned the Alameyin Cinema, Mehmet Avci and Salahaddin Avci, were brutally killed. Approximately 4,000 Turkmen intellectuals and businessman were arrested and sent to unknown prisons, with some never returning.

With no electricity, food or water, the Turkmen experienced

Turkmen corpses that had been buried alive in ditches were unearthed after the massacre in an attempt to identify the bodies.

some of the worst days in Kirkuk's history. The rotten corpses of the Turkmen were all over the city and some were thrown into Hasa-Chay River, which dries out in summer. Birds and wild animals disfigured the corpses on the streets.

As soon as the news of the tragedy spread to other parts of Iraq, Turkmen from Tuz Hurmatu, Tisin, Beshir, and Dakuk tried to enter the city to help their brethren, but were prevented by army units controlled by the Kurds stationed at the city limits. The city of Tuz Hurmatu was also besieged and most of the Turkmen activists there were kept under surveillance, with many being arrested.

The bodies were everywhere. Those hung up as well as those who were desecrated by the animals were difficult to identify. Many of the Kurdish army officers stationed in the Kishlasi with the Second Army Division and Fourth Army Battalion had participated in the massacre. Orders were given by Kirkuk Mayor Maruf Al Barzanji to bury the Turkmen corpses out of the city in an unknown place. As such, a municipality truck driven by Osman Rash, himself a Kurd, took the Turkmen corpses, and they were all put in a long ditch.

Retired colonel Abdullah Abdurrahman was among the most wanted Turkmen in Kirkuk. A reward of 2,000 Iraqi Dinars was offered to bring him either dead or alive, but Abdullah Abdurrahman and his friend Kadir Said Aga had already left the besieged city seeking the assistance of the Iraqi army stationed in Jelawla. He managed to meet Gen. Abdul Karim Kassem in Baghdad. While he was discussing the

Photos of two Turkmen that were hanged on electric posts.

massacre committed against the Turkmen, a swift telex had arrived from the Kurds in Kirkuk informing Kassem that the Turkmen had committed a massacre against the Kurds although Abdulrazzak had already informed the president of the massacre.

Finally, after three bloody days in Kirkuk, the Iraqi army arrived, but the murderers managed to escape to the mountains or were still hiding in the city.

The massacre that began on July 14, 1959 left the city of Kirkuk and the Turkmen people in deep grief and mourning. Most of the Turkmen corpses were gathered and pictured, and the photos were sent to Baghdad before the bodies were taken to a cemetery that would later be renamed the Turkmen Martyrs Cemetery in remembrance of those who died. The city was not yet stabilized and gunshots could be heard in different parts of Kirkuk. In order to control the situation and prevent any revenge, the government outlawed funeral ceremonies, which the Turkmen strongly opposed. News of the killings was heard in Damascus, London, Cairo, Beirut, and Turkey, and the slaughter was loudly condemned in the international media.

Gen. Kassem sent an immediate governmental investigation team to Kirkuk under the command of Gen. Abdurrahman Abdulsattar. Most of the senior army officers testified, including the senior commander Ismail Hammoudi Al Janabi. He declared: "…despite all the warnings sent to Baghdad to prevent the massacre, no reply was received; the Turkmen were the victims and the aggressor Kurds had committed the massacre." As a result of his testimony, Al Janabi's military promotion was stopped and he was forced to resign. General Abdul Karim Kassem condemned the action and reproached those responsible promising severe punishment. He also commanded all Iraqi officers and soldiers to obey "orders issued only from the High Commanding Headquarters."

In the weeks following, President Kassem made several statements and speeches. On July 19, 1959, in front of Saint Joseph Church (Marr Yousuf Church), he promised to bring all of those involved in the massacre to justice. He also issued an arrest warrant against the criminals involved. He declared: "It was very easy for us to crush those who instigated the carnage, hatred and disturbance among the people of Iraq."

During a press conference on July 29, 1959 Kassem stated that the brutal and savage crimes committed in Kirkuk were equal to those committed by Hulagu Khan, grandson of Genghis Khan, who sacked and burned Baghdad in 1258 and executed the last Abbaside caliph. He described the criminals who committed the massacre as being disgraced people and worse than fascists. He also declared, "It is weird that these crimes have been committed by organizations believing in democracy."

During an address in front of the Union of Technical Organizations on August 2, 1959, he declared: "I am not blaming and not intending to deal with any party or ideology that committed these crimes, but I will deal with the individuals who were involved."

When he saw the pictures of disfigured bodies of Turkmen martyrs he was shocked and stated, "I sincerely appreciate the forbearing of my Turkmen brothers and I will do my best to comply. In these days the nation has unified and it will be difficult to be separated."

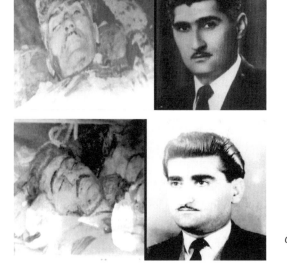

Salahaddin (top) and Mehmet Avci (bottom), Turkmen brothers who owned the Alameyin Cinema in Kirkuk, were both killed in the attack and their cinemas destroyed by artillery fire.

On another occasion he described the Turkmen as the most peaceful nation in Iraq, saying they had suffered a lot. He promised to name one of the TV studios in Baghdad as a Turkmen studio, but it never opened.

A total of 28 criminals, including the mayor of Kirkuk, Maruf Al Barzanji, his brother Hussein Al Barzanji, Abdul-Jabbar Piruz Khan, Majid Hassan and Ata Jemil along with other communist Kurds directly involved were arrested. Many who were involved in the massacre were hiding in Kirkuk and some escaped to Sulaimaniyah. All were sentenced to death. The death penalty was not executed until 1963 when the Arab Nationalists and the Ba'ath Party seized power on February 8, 1963. All the criminals who were involved in the massacre were executed on June 22, 1963 except for Davud Al Janabi, who was executed on February 11, 1963.

During the trial, the mother of one the Turkmen martyrs testified that the Kurds had killed her son because the Kurdish candidate had beaten him in the local elections in Kirkuk. Another witness testified that a Kurdish employee of the Alameyin Cinema and a member of Al Shabiba Union was behind the killing of his employers, brothers Mehmet and Salahaddin Avci.

Those three bloody days in the history of the Turkmen will never be forgotten. However, the Iraqi governments that ruled the country after the massacre, in particular the Ba'ath Party, banned the annual Turkmen martyrs remembrance day of July 14, 1959. Still, it was secretly commemorated by the Turkmen inside Iraq and openly by Turkmen people and organizations abroad.

CASUALTIES OF THE MASSACRE

On July 20, 1959, the head of security in Kirkuk, Nuri Al Khayyat, declared that the number of dead Turkmen was 32, but an additional 20 bodies were buried in an unknown place, which officials were still looking for at the time. Also, several unidentified Turkmen women and children were buried alive. Some bodies were identified but others would be reburied with no names. General Abdul Karim Kassem officially declared on August 2, 1959 that 79 Turkmen were killed, but he later changed that number to 31, claiming that some of the pictures had been duplicated.

Hydro facilities, telephone lines and main water pipes were destroyed. Thousands of Turkmen homes, businesses and shops throughout the city were ransacked and destroyed, including 120 large units and warehouses. Hundreds of Turkmen were wounded with 130 listed in serious condition, and others dissapeared never to return. More than 3,000 Turkmen were arrested.

TURKMEN MARTYRED ON JULY 14, 1959
1. Ata Hayrullah – major-colonel
2. Ihsan Hayrullah – lieutenant-colonel
3. Salahaddin Avci – businessman
4. Mehmet Avci – civil servant
5. Cihat Mukhtar – teacher
6. Nihat Mukhtar – teacher
7. Emel Fuad Mukhtar – student
8. Ali Nafitchi – businessman
9. Kasim Nafitchi – businessman
10. Zuheyir Izzet Cayci – café owner
11. Siddik Reza – worker
12. Cahit Fahrattin – civil servant
13. Fethullah Yunus – oilfield technician
14. Cuma Kamber – technician
15. Enver Abbas – student
16. Kazim Bektas – student
17. Sakir Zeynel – café owner

 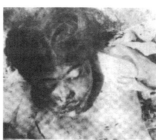

Emel Mukhtar was only 13 when she was killed on July 14, 1959. The photo on the far left was taken in 1958.

18. Osman Hidir – café owner
19. Haji Nazim – independent student
20. Hasp Ali – employee
21. Ibrahim Ramadan – auto technician
22. Gain Naked – employee
23. Adel Abdulhamit – employee
24. Kemal Abdulsamad – engineer
25. Abdulhalik Ismail – student
26. Abdullah Ahmet Beyatli – technician
27. Salahaddin Kayaci – employee
28. Selah Terzi – tailor
29. Abbas Kadir – student
30. Ibrahim Hamza – butcher
31. Selah Kopurlu – police officer
32. Nurettin Aziz – employee
33. Kemal Abulsamad's mother – housewife
34. Halil ? – self-employed

According to Marion Farouk-Sluglett and Peter Sluglett in their article "Kirkuk, July 1959: Iraq since 1958 – From Revolution to Dictatorship":

"Even more than the Mosul battles, much of the fighting at Kirkuk was only incidentally concerned with party politics; it was far more profoundly rooted in the deep-seated antagonism between the original Turkmen population of the city and the more recent Kurdish incomers. The ICP (Iraqi Communist Party) had considerable support among the Kurds, while the Turkmen, who were generally both better

 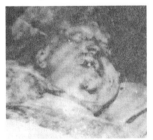

Osman Hidir, a Turkmen café owner, before and after being brutally murdered in the riot.

off and more conservative politically, were united by ethnic solidarity rather than party affiliation. Since the end of 1958, a number of sensitive appointments in the city had been granted to the Kurds, with the result that the Turkmen, who had always dominated the socio-economic and political life of the town, now left them increasingly at a disadvantage. It is unclear who started the fighting – apparently over the route of the procession to celebrate the first anniversary of the Revolution – but the result was that between 31 and 79 people were killed, most of them Turkmen."

Despite all the incidents and the massacre of July 14, 1959, the Turkmen were able to reorganize themselves and decided to continue to live with the Kurds.

THE SITUATION BETWEEN 1963 AND 1968

The unstable situation of the Turkmen after the massacre of July 14, 1959 was gradually tightening up despite the slow healing of the wounds felt by the community. The Arab Nationalists and the Ba'ath Party had overthrown Gen. Abdul Karim Kassem and seized power.

The Turkmen were pleased with the revolution of 1963, that ended the rule of Abdul Karim Kassem who had done little for the Turkmen after the massacre of July 14, 1959. Many Turkmen military personnel were part of the Revolutionary Committee. While celebrating the revolution in Kirkuk, they were preparing to send 2,000 Turkmen to participate in the public convention celebrating the first month of the revolution in Baghdad to support the new government. An appointment was given to the Turkmen delegation to meet the new Iraqi president, Abdul Salam Arif, and his prime minister, Ahmet Hassan Albakir, in the presidential palace in the Al Kesra region of Baghdad (Abdulsalam Arif represented the Arab Nationalist Party and Ahmet Hassan Albakir represented the Ba'ath Party).

During the meeting in the presidential palace, the Turkmen faced a few difficulties. First of all, for security reasons it was difficult to transfer the Turkmen convoy of 2,000 people in front of the Turkmen Fraternity Club (Kardashlik) in the Al Awaziyya region to the presidential palace. Upon arriving at the presidential palace, the Turkmen came face to face with the Kurdish delegation that was led by the mayor of Kirkuk, Fazil Al Talabani, who was joined by four other Kurds.

Fazil Al Talabani had been appointed without election by the Communist Party in Kirkuk during the massacre. The Turkmen were uncomfortable with the situation because the meeting was supposed to have been a private encounter with the prime minister and his advisors to discuss the situation in Kirkuk. The request of the Kurds to meet the president at the same time was an awkward attempt to change the identity of the Turkmen city of Kirkuk. The Kurdish delegation left the palace quietly without further difficulties.

However, when the Turkmen delegation went to meet the prime minister, matters became uncomfortable when Rahmatallah Albayati, a pro-communist lawyer, insisted on being part of the Turkmen delegation. When the names of those selected to meet the prime minister were announced and Rahmatallah Albayati was not among them, he was asked to leave the palace. The delegation to meet the prime minister and some of his cabinet ministers included Nurettin Alwaiz, a lawyer appointed as a spokesperson during the meeting; Dr. Mardan Ali; Colonel Abdullah Abdurrahman; Abdulkadir Suleyman; Necmettin Izzettin; Izzettin Kocawa, a businessman; and Ata Terzibashi, a lawyer.

During the meeting, the Turkmen delegation presented a list of their anxieties to the prime minister and asked for the following resolutions:

1. The execution of the Kurds who had participated in the July 14 massacre. The execution order had been issued during the tenure of Abdul Karim Kassem, but it had not been carried out.

2. The Kurdish families who had recently settled in Kirkuk should return to their previous area in the north. Thousands of Kurds had migrated to Kirkuk looking for a better life and also to avoid the fighting in the north taking place between the different Kurdish factions. The Kurds had benefited under the rule of former Kirkuk mayor Maruf Al Barzanji, who had encouraged their immigration and also issued title

deeds to Kurds who had illegally built their homes on the outskirts of the city in such regions as Shorija and Raheem Awa.

3. The Turkmen should repossess the land that had been redistributed by Al Barzanji.

4. Political, administrative and cultural rights should be granted to the Turkmen.

5. The Turkmen should have an active role in the newly formed Ba'athist government.

Sadly, the Turkmen's requests were not considered. It did not take long for the Ba'ath Party to begin exerting its authority. After thousands of people were jailed and executed, the Turkmen people realized that this revolution would be no different than the governments that had ruled Iraq in the past. Of all the resolutions asked by the Turkmen, only one issue brought a sense of justice to the families of those killed on July 14, 1959 – the execution of the participants in the Kirkuk massacre.

THE BA'ATH ERA, 1968-2003

The meaning of the Ba'ath Party, founded and established by Michael Aflak and Salah Bitar in Syria-Damascus 1943, was translated to "The Socialist Party for Arab Resurrection." The party seized power in Syria and Iraq in 1963, but lasted only six months in Iraq. The Arab Nationalists successfully overthrew the Ba'ath regime, but they only stayed in power for a short time as the Ba'ath Party regained power on July 17, 1968.

Iraqi President Abdul Rahman Arif had surrendered to the army units, which had surrounded the presidential palace in Baghdad. A few months later, the toppled president was exiled to Turkey and Ahmet Hassan Albakir became the new president of Iraq.

Although Saddam Hussein was the second man in the Ba'ath Party, he was the one ruling the country, using the president as a puppet. Saddam Hussein was successful in eliminating his competitors and the followers of President Albakir such as Hardan Al Tikriki, Abdulrazzak Al Nayif, Hammad Shihab, Abulhalik Alsamarraea, Murtatha Alhadithi and many others. He then started to control both the army and the Revolutionary Command of the Ba'ath Party.

On July 17, 1979, Saddam seized power after the death of Albakir's eldest son, Muhammed, who was killed in a bizarre accident. Saddam banned Albakir from all of his military and political authorities and announced himself as the new president of Iraq. A few years later, Albakir was found dead in his house; the cause of death was left unknown. Many people from Albakir's family and his supporters were jailed or went missing. Saddam Hussein trusted no one in this matter. He even ordered his own half-brothers, Watban and Barzan, under house arrest in order to prevent any family dispute over ruling the country.

Despite the initial objective of the Ba'ath Party to create a socialist Arab culture, the society was manipulated to serve and protect only the rights of the Arabs who belonged to the party and, in particular, the interests of Saddam Hussein.

When the Ba'ath Party took charge in July 1968, what followed were some of the most tragic days for the Turkmen. Under Saddam's orders, Turkmen and other minorities were arrested, jailed without trial, and executed. Many disappeared with no record. Yet the world was unaware of the situation in Iraq.

After the 1991 Gulf War, the international community continued to disregard the plight of the Turkmen in Kirkuk, Diyalah, Salahaddin, Mosul, and Erbil. Despite the fact that the cities of Kirkuk and

Saddam Hussein became president of Iraq on July 17, 1979 after the mysterious death of Ahmet Hassan Albakir. Saddam earned a notorious reputation before being forcibly removed in 2003.

Sulaimaniyah were both located south of the 36th parallel and Mosul was in the no-fly-zone, only Sulaimaniyah was put under international protection. However, Kirkuk and other Turkmen regions remained under the hostilities of the Ba'ath regime.

ARABIFICATION AND ITS EFFECT ON THE TURKMEN
The Ba'ath regime had implemented an Arabification policy and gradually intensified the repression of the Turkmen. The following are examples of atrocities committed against the Turkmen people of Iraq under Saddam Hussein's rule:

1. Nihat Fazil Dakuklu was executed. Born in the small Turkmen township of Dakuk (Tavuk) located 47 kilometres south of Kirkuk, Nihat Fazil Dakuklu, like other Turkmen colleagues, had demonstrated to have the Turkmen's legitimate rights recognized. Despite being a member of the Iraqi army who had served faithfully for his country, he was cruelly tortured shortly after his arrest and was executed on January 2, 1969.

2. Mehmet Fatih Saatchi (*pictured at left*) was shot dead in Kirkuk. On July 7, 1970, a hot summer day in Kirkuk, a group of secret military members of the Ba'ath regime with some pro-Ba'athist Arabs had entered a small café at the outskirts of the Citadel of Kirkuk. Their aim was to create unrest in the Grand Bazaar of Kirkuk.

One member of the group had asked the café owner to serve him food and drink. After a short delay, the man insisted that Mehmet Fatih Saatchi, who was sitting with a friend, serve him. An argument started and within seconds Saatchi, the family's only son, was shot dead.

The Turkmen were shocked when they heard the ugly news. Consequently, the Grand Bazaar was closed and all Turkmen in Kirkuk announced a two-day strike. More than 60,000 Turkmen men, women and children participated in the funeral, which turned into a demonstration calling for revenge and demanding that those responsible be brought to justice.

In response, the Ba'ath government brought thousands of troops to the area in the Musalla district to suppress an anticipated conflict and to protect the pro-Ba'thist Arabs.

3. The execution of Dr. Nizameddin Arif (*pictured at right*), a prominent Turkmen leader. Born in the Piryadi district of Kirkuk in 1927, he was the second child of Arif Agas, the headman of Piryadi district. Nizameddin Arif returned to Iraq after completing a PhD in agricultural economy in Turkey. He then became a general inspector in  the directorate of Agriculture in Kirkuk and was later promoted to a general director in the Ministry of Agriculture in Baghdad. After working hard in his field, he was nominated as the minister of Agriculture in Abdul Rahman Arif's cabinet.

His family had financially supported him during the first year of his studies and after that the National Union of the Turkmen Students in Turkey granted him a scholarship. The Ba'ath Party was not pleased to see highly educated Turkmen in the Ministry of Agriculture, and steps were taken to remove him. He was accused of being a spy for Turkey and was among 51 other Iraqis who were hanged publicly from the gallows set up in the Liberation Square in Baghdad on January 20, 1970. His death was a clear warning for the Turkmen in Iraq and Turkmen students abroad. Consequently, most of the Turkmen graduates abroad, especially in Turkey, refused to return to Iraq.

Dr. Nizameddin Arif was executed for many reasons:

> A) He was accused for being a Turkmen chauvinist;
>
> B) He received a scholarship to study in Turkey;
>
> C) He was involved in political activities in Turkey and became a member of the Iraqi Turkmen Association established in Istanbul in 1958;
>
> D) He helped establish the Kardashlik (Turkmen Fraternity Club) in Baghdad;
>
> E) He assisted in getting many Turkmen employed in the agriculture directorate in Kirkuk.

4. In 1972 the Ba'ath Party issued orders to public banks to stop

giving credit to Turkmen businessmen.

5. The Ba'ath Party reduced the Turkmen employee numbers in the Iraqi Petroleum Company; by 1972, only 500 of the IPC's 10,000 employees were Turkmen.

6. As part of Saddam's Arabification policy, Turkmen graduates were refused employment in Kirkuk and were sent to the southern regions. Only Arabs and Kurds were employed in Kirkuk and other Turkmen regions.

7. On December 1, 1972, Jafer Reza Arafat, a Turkmen farmer in the village of Selamiye near Mosul was executed for unknown reasons.

8. The Baghdad government sent most of its conscripted Turkmen soldiers and army personnel to the front lines during the Iraq-Iran War, which lasted approximately eight years.

9. On January 2, 1980 the Revolutionary Command under Decree 1391 issued orders to establish the project of building new dwellings to accommodate over 20,000 Turkmen in the southern Al Samawa, Kut, Al Nasiriyyah and Al Basra provinces. The project was abandoned due to the Iraq-Iran War.

10. More than 500 Turkmen youth and prominent Turkmen from the neighborhood of Tisin in Kirkuk were executed. Agriculture technician Jem Al Jabbar, teacher Salah Hasan and lawyer Ali Ekber Rauf were exposed to the same end.

11. In 1981 two people with Ahmet Reshid Bayatlı were executed from the Karatay village of Mosul.

12. Major Halit Sait Akkoyunlu, prominent teacher Mehmet Korkmaz, Rushdu Reshat Muhtar, İzzettin Celil Abdulhamit, Selahattin Abdullah Tenekechi, Selahattin Necim Hattat, Muhsin Ali,

Cevdet Avci (left); Mehmet Korkmaz (centre); Halit Shengul (right).

Mustafa Mehmet Abbas and Hamit Rahman were executed between 1980-1983.

13. In November 1985, a curfew was imposed in Kirkuk and an operation to search Turkmen houses was held by the military forces. Many Turkmen dwellings in the Citadel of Kirkuk were destroyed and the Turkmen occupants arrested.

14. In January 1981, the prominent Turkmen teachers Halit Shengul and Abdulkerim Allahverdi were executed.

15. Cevdet Avci, a correspondent for *Kardaslik* magazine, was arrested on October 10, 1981. Since no news was ever heard from him, it is believed that he was executed and the body not delivered to the family.

16. In 1981 the following Turkmen intellectuals from several different Turkmen regions were executed:

> Selim Hamdi Bakir – a teacher from Tuz Hurmatu
> Hashim Hamdi Baki – a student from Tuz Hurmatu
> Abbas Nazli – agriculture technician
> Ali Abdulvahit – a teacher from Beshir
> Hidir Ali Merdan – a teacher from Tisin
> Sefil Mehdi Gaip – a teacher from Tisin
> Zeynelabidin Sabir – electric engineer from Tisin
> Ahmet Mehmet Ali – a teacher from Tisin executed in 1982
> Ali Murat Hussein – a teacher from Tisin executed in 1982
> Necat Kasım Koryalı – traffic policeman
> Mehmet Hussein – a student from Beshir

17. The borders of the predominantly Turkmen province of Kirkuk and Diyalah were changed:

> A) In January 29, 1976 under the Revolutionary Command Decree 41 Subject 4, Article 159 the laws of provinces, the largest district of Kirkuk Tuz Hurmatu, located 75 kilometres south of Kirkuk and 132 kilometres from Tikrit, was annexed to the newly-formed Salahaddin province. Under the same decree, the Turkmen name of Kirkuk was changed to Al Tameem. Similarly, the district of Kifri was annexed to

the province of Diyalah and Chamchamal was annexed to Sulaimaniyah.

B) The total area of Kirkuk, which was the fourth largest province of Iraq, was reduced from 19,543 km^2 to 9,426 km^2. Consequently Kirkuk became the 14th largest province of Iraq.

C) On September 11, 1989, according to the Revolutionary Command Decree 434, Articles 4, 5, 6 laws of provinces, the region of Altun Kopru was annexed to the province of Erbil. Altun Kopru was re-annexed to Kirkuk after the uprising of 1991.

D) On July 26, 1987 according to the Revolutionary Command Decree 459, Article 5 revised laws of provinces No. 196 in 1969, the district of Mendeli in Diyalah province was changed to the region of Mendeli. Under the same decree the region of Baladrooz was changed to the district of Baladrooz and the region of Mendeli was annexed to the district of Baladrooz. (The administration system of Iraq follows the following order: village, region, district, city and province.)

18. Turkmen villages were officially changed to Arabic revolutionary names such as;

Original Turkmen Names	Arabic Names
Altun Kopru	Al Nahrain
Kara Incir	Al Rabia
Shirince Bulak	Al Yarmook
Tercil	Al Kadisiyya
Yengice	Abu Muhaynan
Tokmaklu	Al Hansaa
Buyuk (Grand) Sari Tepe	Al Raou
Kuchuk (little) Sari Tepe	Al Waleed
Yarimca	Jedda
Karali	Rehtad
Zindana	Misir

19. The names of Turkmen soccer teams and sport clubs were also given Arabic names.

20. Turkmen streets, quarters and wards were changed to Arabic names, such as:

Original Turkmen Names	Arabic Names
Avchi	Hay Al Zawra
Pamukchular	Hay Al Mansoor
Korya Bazaar	Al Baath Bazar
Chukur	Hay Al Arap
Tabakchali Bridge	Al Kaed Bridge
Yeni Tisin	Tisin Al Jadeeda

Many new wards were built, such as Hay Al Baath near Tisin, Mutasam, Al-Asra, Nasir, Karama Muthanna, Al-Shuhada, Al-Wasiti, Badir, Milad, Girnata, Adan and 1-Adar.

21. At the end of November 1993, following the uprising of 1991, Turkmen individuals who participated in the revolt were targeted and their families were deported from Kirkuk.

22. According to a special report of the Human Rights Commission of the United Nations, over 25,000 Turkmen Shiite families were apparently relocated to other places. These families were mainly from Tisin quarter, which was completely demolished in the beginning of 1980.

Ayman Jabbar (left) and Sevinc Mohammed Mimaroglu (centre) were killed. Zehra Bektas (right) set herself on fire to protest the atrocities committed against her people in the city of Kirkuk.

23. A young Turkmen woman named Ayman Jabbar was taken from her home on April 11, 1991. She was accused of cheering during the uprising of 1991. Saddam Hussein executed her father, Jabbar Kushunchu, in the 1970s. Ayman's pro-Ba'athist Arab neighbor informed the security forces of her involvement after they suppressed the uprising of April 26, 1991. Ayman was shot dead with many other Turkmen near an army barrack in Tuz Hurmatu on April 15, 1991. Her body was later found in a mass grave in 2003 along with 45 other Turkmen corpses.

24. Sevinc Mohammed Mimaroglu, a mother of five children, lost her life after her husband Asad Resit Zeynel, an officer in the Iraqi army, was sentenced to life imprisonment. She was one of Saddam's victims.

25. Many Turkmen women were executed in Kirkuk, Telafer and Tuz Hurmatu under different accusations: Suriye Mohammed, Belkis Hamit Abdullah, Nahida Kanber Cayirli, Aynur Hamit Mustafa were all from Tuz Hurmatu and Zeynep Tisinli was from the Tisin district.

26. Seyid Halil Telaferli and his pregnant wife were executed in 1986 in Baghdad.

27. Another Turkmen woman, Zehra Bektas, set herself on fire when the Iraqi intelligence services raided her house and forced her family to leave Kirkuk. She was badly beaten up along with her father

---

BELOW: Long-standing Turkmen houses in Old Tisin were destroyed by the Iraqi army to make way for the construction of roads and railways.
OPPOSITE PAGE: An old church in Kirkuk was also hit.

who also resisted leaving. She sacrificed herself for the Turkmen city of Kirkuk. The family was expelled to Erbil after her death.

DESTRUCTION OF TURKMEN AREAS
The Ba'ath Party had put immense pressure on the Turkmen of Kirkuk and its vicinity. In order to establish military facilities in the north, many Turkmen villages and small towns were evacuated and then destroyed. Beside some of the evacuated villages pro-regime Arabs from the south would settle. A harsh Arabification policy was implemented by the regime to dilute the Turkmen population in Kirkuk. As a result, over 2,000 Turkmen dwellings were destroyed, mainly in Musalla, Tisin, Hamzeli, Mahatta, Hay Al Zubbat, Gavurbagi, Sahat Tayaran and Almas. The Muhammediye Mosque in Sahat Al Tayaran as well as the old church in the Citadel of Kirkuk were destroyed.

Eski Tisin (the Old Tisin) was the largest district in Kirkuk and it was completely decimated. More than 1,500 Turkmen houses that reflected the old Turkmen architecture were destroyed. Train stations and highways were built instead. An estimated 25,000 Turkmen residents from Old Tisin were forced to settle in different parts of Kirkuk without compensation and many were exiled either to Beni Slawa camp in Erbil or to the south of Iraq. Many Turkmen villages were totally destroyed under false pretenses. For example, the village of Bulawa was destroyed for being close to the military airport

in Kirkuk. However, an Arab dwelling next to it was exempted. The Turkmen villages of Beshir, Badawa, Topzawa, Yaychi, Turk Alan, Kumbetler, Kizliyar and Tokmakli were all destroyed.

CULTURAL RIGHTS FOR MINORITIES DECLARED
In order to soothe the ethnic groups in Iraq and particularly the Turkmen, a declaration of cultural rights for minorities came into effect on January 24, 1970. The intention was to cut ties between the Turkmen in Iraq and other Turkish cultures outside the country. The second reason was to emphasize that the Turkmen language spoken in Iraq was not synonymous with the Turkish language in Turkey. To do this, the old Turkmen language with the Arabic alphabet was forcibly imposed. Some other aspects of these rights included:

1. Turkmen students were allowed to study their language at elementary schools.

2. Some school names were changed to Turkmen names, such as Dede Hirji Elementary School, and Çiçek Elementary School.

3. Turkmen poets, writers and teachers began to form curriculum committees to prepare the subjects.

4. The Turkmen Literary Union was established.

5. Monthly and weekly Turkmen publications were allowed such as *Kardaslık* ("Fraternity" magazine).

6. Turkmen poets and writers were allowed to publish their books. However, when they began to express their feelings about cultural freedom and how it related to the Turkmen people, they were soon seen by the ruling Ba'ath Party as radicals. Many were arrested and sentenced to life in prison, and others were executed. Muhammed "Izzet" Hattat and Hassan Gorem (a blind poet) were both sentenced to seven years in prison and died shortly after their release as a result of the torture they had suffered. Ismail Sertturkmen, the writer of the Turkmen national anthem (with Olsun Mavi Asmanim Sana) and publisher of the first Turkmen sport magazine in Kirkuk, was jailed for writing a children's book called *Homesick*, after the content of the book was interpreted into different political meanings. Subsequently, the Iraqi security collected all of his books from the Turkmen schools

and bookstores and burned them in front of his eyes.

7. The Turkmen program period in Kirkuk Television was extended.

8. The Directorate of Cultural Affairs was formed under the Ministry of Information and Cultural Affairs.

Although the 1970 declaration said the cultural rights of Iraq's minorities would be enhanced, this new environment did not last long for the Turkmen. The Ba'ath Party gradually began to cut subsidies to Turkmen schools, forcing parents to financially support education and school activities. The Ba'ath Party also appointed some unpopular party sympathizers as directors of cultural and educational institutions. The appointees were functioning for the party's benefit. Families of Arab students collected signatures opposing the teaching in the Turkmen language. The Arab tribesmen living in the Turkmen districts then forwarded the petition to the authorities in Kirkuk.

ELIMINATION OF THE TURKMEN'S CULTURAL RIGHTS

The Cultural Rights for Minorities lasted almost two years and then were eliminated altogether. After an order was issued by the Iraqi government, the following changes were made to the cultural rights of the Turkmen:

1. Turkmen students were forced to restudy in Arabic.

2. The Turkmen publications and newspapers were ordered to appear half in Arabic and half in Turkmen language using Arabic script.

3. The Turkmen school names had to be changed to Arabic revo-

FAR LEFT: *Muhammed Hattat, a respected Turkmen writer, was tortured in prison.*
LEFT: *All of the books written by Ismail Sertturkmen were burned.*

lutionary names, such as:

Former Turkmen Names	New Arabic Names
Yildizlar Al Fajr	Al Jadeed
Dede Hijri	Kasim Al Thakafi
Yedi Kardesh	Al Baath
Kara Altun	8 February
Mutlu	Al Nasr
Shanli	That Alsawaree
Dogruluk	Omer bin Abdulzaiz
24 Ocak	Usama bin Zeyd
AK Tash	Al Mutanabbi
İleri Ibn	Al Haythem

4. Many Turkmen teachers were either arrested or exiled.

5. Turkmen books were collected and destroyed.

6. Families who had subsidized the Turkmen curriculum were interrogated and many were arrested.

7. As the pressure gradually increased, Turkmen students in Kirkuk staged a boycott, protesting the Ba'ath Party. Turkmen students refused to attend schools and had gathered in front of the buildings to show their anger and frustration. The Ba'ath Party started to use force and special forces began arresting the students and teachers. Firearms were used and many students were shot. Many of those wounded refused to be treated in the government hospital and the city of Kirkuk was in chaos.

On the first day of the boycott, Huseyin Ali Demirci (*pictured at left*), a famous Turkmen artist who was successful in the Tembel Abbas television series, was arrested. Two days later, on October 24, 1971, he was dead. He had been tied to an electrical pole near his home. The assassination of Hussein Ali Demirci was a clear message to the Turkmen students that they would face the same consequence if they continued their course of action. After three days the student boycott was terminated.

VIOLATION OF THE TURKMEN'S RIGHTS

1. The Turkmen students were prohibited to study in their language, and instead were forced to learn in Arabic.

2. Speaking Turkmen was banned in governmental buildings. Teachers speaking this language were exiled to the south and students were dismissed from school for three months.

3. In a secret memorandum to Saddam Hussein, Kirkuk Education Director Izzettin Sardar stated he had exiled Turkmen teachers and artists to the south.

4. Speaking the Turkmen language in public places was declared to be an offence. As such, mosque clerks were forced to deliver their Friday sermons in Arabic. Government officials prepared these sermons and the clerics were forced to praise the Ba'ath regime and Saddam Hussein. All Turkmen clerics were forced to speak in Arabic.

5. After repeated warnings, Haji Hadi Mosque Cleric Molla Mahmood was arrested and tortured for disobeying the order to speak Arabic. Imam Mehdi Boyaci, a 70-year-old cleric for Dakuk mosque, was also ordered to deliver his Friday sermons in Arabic, but he refused. As a result, he was taken from the mosque by the intelligence service and was found dead near Habbaniya Lake 40 days later with several torture marks on his body. The young students in Dakuk attempted to demonstrate against the tyranny, but were all arrested and many were executed. Some corpses of the Turkmen students from Dakuk were delivered to their families and the cost of the execution as well as transportation fees was collected in return. On top of that, the families of the students were transferred to the south.

6. Turkmen school names were changed to Arabic names and Ba'athist political studies were imposed.

7. Turkmen high school students were forced to study the Kurdish language as a subject in grades 11 and 12.

8. The Arabs who were brought from the south replaced most of the Turkmen teachers, principals and vice principals.

9. Most of the Turkmen teachers and education staff were transferred to the south.

10. Turkmen teachers over the age of 45 were forced to enter early retirement without benefits.

11. Mandatory military training was imposed outside the Turkmen settlements for teachers and students during the summer holidays. This was to prevent Turkmen student gatherings during this time.

12. Severe punishments were imposed against teachers who refused to attend summer military training. Many teachers were transferred to the south and students were dismissed from school.

13. The Ba'ath Student Union was able to arrest Turkmen students and teachers under false charges.

14. Many Turkmen teachers and students were arrested and some were executed without trial based on false charges.

15. The best training opportunities were given to the Arab students.

16. In order to prevent the Turkmen students from participating in the final exams, security forces had entered their classrooms to arrest them.

17. Arab students were given high marks to facilitate their acceptance in the universities.

18. Only Arab students were accepted in the army colleges.

19. Only Arab students could be exempted from mandatory military service after graduation.

20. Only Arab students were permitted to continue postgraduate studies while the Turkmen graduates were sent for mandatory military service.

21. Arab students who did not have the option of postgraduate studies turned out to be army officers with all reserved privileges.

22. Turkmen were deprived of press freedom. Most of their newspapers and magazines were cancelled and they were forced to use the Arabic alphabet.

23. Abdullah Abdurrahman, a retired colonel and the chairman of the Turkmen Fraternity Hearth in Baghdad, and his friends, associate professor Nejdet Kocak, Dr. Reza Demirci, and businessman Adil Serif, were all arrested and later executed on January 16, 1980.

24. Houses were searched for any form of Turkmen publications. Thousands of such books were destroyed.

25. Many Turkmen leaders and intellectuals (teachers and businessmen) were assassinated.

Turkmen dwellings in the Citadel of Kirkuk (opposite page) were destroyed (below) by Iraqi army artillery.

26. The Turkmen TV broadcasting period was minimized to only 30 minutes a day.

27. More than 500 Turkmen from the destroyed township of Old Tisin were executed.

28. Turkmen houses and lands were expropriated and granted to newcomers (pro-Saddam Arabs).

29. Turkmen were forced to change their ethnicity to Arab during the 1978 census.

30. Turkmen houses were confiscated and freely given to Arabs that arrived from the south.

31. The rules governing the transaction of immovable property in Kirkuk were altered so the Turkmen were not allowed to purchase these assets.

32. Turkmen were allowed to sell their immovable properties only to the Arabs after obtaining Ba'ath Party consent.

33. Many Turkmen females were forcibly married to the Arabs and some were raped and executed.

34. In order to change the demographical shape of the Turkmen areas, the Arab bridegrooms married to Turkmen received marriage allowances of around 10,000 Iraqi Dinars (roughly $33,000 US).

35. Turkmen gatherings were prevented during the weekends.

36. Turkmen who regularly attended prayers in the mosques were arrested and sentenced to different terms.

37. Business credits were disallowed to the Turkmen businessmen and farmers.

38. Turkmen graduates from the Petroleum Training Center and engineering department were not allowed to have jobs at Iraqi

Colonel Nejat Shukru (far left), General Omer Ali, Lt.-Col. Aydin Mustafa (left).

Petroleum Company (IPC) in Kirkuk. Most of the Turkmen employees and engineers were forced either to early retirement or transferred to the cities of Basra and Beiji.

39. The 5,000-year-old Citadel of Kirkuk was destroyed.

40. Arab families were settled in almost every street in Kirkuk and began spying on Turkmen families. They would report false statements against their neighbours to the security forces

41. Arab families who agreed to settle in the farmlands outside of Kirkuk obtained additional credits and farm equipment.

42. The prominent Turkmen intellectual Fatih Shakir Kazim, who had been sentenced for 20 years imprisonment, died in the Abu Ghraib prison in 1990. Enver Mahmut Neftchi also died in this prison in January 1993.

43. Hundreds of Turkmen were left in different prisons under extremely unhealthy conditions.

44. Abbas Mehdi Riza Bender, Isam Sarikahya and Hussein Safi Sultan were executed in February 1993 under false charges.

45. Tahsin Korkmaz, a 24-year-old Turkmen student, was executed on April 21, 1993.

46. Turkmen senior army officers and personnel were assassinated (Col. Nejat Shukru, Maj.-Gen. Omer Ali, Lt.-Col. Aydin Mustafa, 1st Lt. Ahmet Kasapoglu, Gen. Ismet Saber, Lt.-Col. Halit Akkoyunlu and many others).

FREEDOM AND DEMOCRACY FOR ALL

The Turkmen are one of the main elements of Iraq besides the Arabs and Kurds. They have sincerely contributed in various aspects to the

1st Lt. Ahmet Kasapoglu (right), General Ismet Saber, Lt.-Col. Halit Akkoyunlu (far right).

development of the country. Despite the fact that the very first article of the United Nations Universal Declaration of Human Rights says all "human beings are born free and equal in dignity and rights" and "are endowed with reason and conscience and should act towards one another in a spirit of brotherhood," this attitude was never conveyed towards the Turkmen. They have been subjected to various acts of discrimination and deprived of basic human rights since the formation of the State of Iraq in 1921.

The Turkmen are a well-educated nation that strongly believes in freedom and democracy. They protected and served Iraq throughout the country's history. They also stood for Iraqi land and national integrity. They always demanded the other Iraqi segments rights and called all Iraqis to live in peace and harmony. The Turkmen were never involved in armed rebellion against the former Iraqi governments. Although some Iraqi segments considered this as a weak point, the Turkmen always believed that their strength was generated by not believing in violence and bloodshed. They strongly believe that everyone is entitled to all legitimate rights and freedom without any distinctions based on race, colour, sex, language, religion, politics, national or social origin, property, birth, or other status. Furthermore, they always sought peaceful solutions to keep the integrity of Iraq. They were a part of the Peace Monitoring Force (PMF) formed by the American, British and Turkish governments to prevent the fight between the Kurdistan Democratic Party (KDP) and the Patriotic Union of Kurdistan (PUK).

In the late 1970s, Jalal Talabani, leader of the Patriotic Union of Kurdistan, had received the support of President Saddam Hussein. In 2005, Talabani would later become president of Iraq.

However, three million Turkmen were always denied by the former Iraqi government while the Kurds, who never stopped struggling since the end of the First World War, were given an autonomous region and their rights were stated in the former Iraqi constitutions. Article 6 of the Iraqi constitution, which was adopted on July 7, 1990, reads:

"The people of Iraq are consisted of Arabs and Kurds. The constitution recognizes the national rights of the Kurds; within the framework of integrity of the country, the State and people, ensures the legitimate rights of all Iraqis."

The Turkmen had participated in all former opposition meetings held in the United States, Britain, Salahaddin and many other countries. The Iraqi Turkmen Front was the sole representative for the three million Turkmen who live in Iraq who always stood against proposals aimed at dividing the state. The Turkmen as a nation are strictly devoted to their country and ethics. Yet for some reason, priorities have been given to the Kurds, Shiites and recently to the Sunnis, leaving the Turkmen to face their destiny.

AFTER THE TOPPLING OF SADDAM HUSSEIN

The Turkmen people of Iraq had strongly believed that the time had come for all Iraqis to disregard the remnants of political dispute instigated by the former regime and focus on the future. As such, in this difficult time it is consistently required from all Iraqis to act perceptively and put the emphasis on unity and conciliation in working together to shield the country and the region from the danger of corruption and dissension.

Yet, once again the political rights of the Turkmen were violated in the same way as in past Iraqi regimes. A telling example of this was how representatives from the Iraqi Turkmen Front were not consulted during the creation of the Iraqi Interim Council.

ABSENCE OF TURKMEN FROM IRAQI INTERIM COUNCIL

The idea of forming the Iraqi Interim Council had satisfied most Iraqis and particularly the Turkmen, who felt this was one of the first major steps towards democracy. It was a preliminary stage in commencing a strong political foundation in building the future government of Iraq. Despite all the declared resolutions of the opposition meetings in Salahaddin and London that said, "representatives of all Iraqi political parties and groups should be represented in any future council in Iraq," the ITF was deliberately excluded. When the majority of Iraqi party leaders met to form the Iraqi Interim Council on July 13, 2003, the ITF leader was left out of the discussions.

As such, we strongly believe that this failure will ultimately lead to corruption, unrest and, eventually, dissension in near future. In denying the Turkmen access, some groups are trying to cast suspicion on our loyalty to Iraq and lessen our influence in drawing the future of the state and the region.

We also believe there are several other motivations behind this decision. First of all, the accessibility of natural resources, particularly gas and oil, in the Turkmen region – predominantly in Kirkuk, Khanakin, Mosul and surrounding areas – is the main cause for the aggression applied against us in our homeland. Without listening to the views of the Turkmen, the secret agreements and maneuvers applied by some powerful political parties will destabilize the region and cause more bloodshed in the future.

Beyond that, despite the Iraqi Turkmen Front's participation in all opposition meetings in London, Washington and Salahaddin, only one unfamiliar and non-political Turkmen candidate was appointed. In the meantime, the Kurds gained six seats. Three Kurdish party leaders as well as an Arab political party leader were all appointed in the council. For the Turkmen, Mrs. Songul Chabuk was appointed as a representative.

THE FALLOUT AFTER APRIL 10, 2003

During the United States' Operation *IRAQI FREEDOM,* which began in March 2003, thousands of Kurdish militias (known as peshmerga) poured into Kirkuk and proclaimed the city as the heart of so-called Kurdistan. Upon entering Kirkuk, the Kurds committed the following actions:

1. Their first target was to destroy and set fire to the city's land registry and population registry offices as well as the main municipality building. Thousands of dossiers, stamps and data related to the Turkmen presence in Kirkuk were stolen and, in some cases, replaced by false documents. The original unused national identity cards and passports were also stolen. The Kurds applied similar tactics during the 1991 uprising.

2. Kurdish flags were raised over government buildings and public places.

3. Large numbers of private and government buildings were looted and burned. Hundreds of vehicles including buses and farm equipment along with other stolen goods and medical instruments were sent to Sulaimaniyah and Erbil. Homes, businesses, hotels, stores, and warehouses were looted and set ablaze.

4. The historical Kirkuk Kishlasi, which housed the Turkmen Folklore Centre, was looted and destroyed.

5. The stolen unused national identity cards were given to the Kurds who arrived from other provinces (Sulaimaniyah, Erbil and Zaho), Iran, and Turkey and were registered as inhabitants of Kirkuk. The newcomers settled in the houses of Arabs that were forcibly evicted and high-ranking Ba'ath Party members who fled the city before the fall of Saddam.

6. A group of PUK flag-waving peshmergas opened fire on a Turkmen group gathered in front of the Turkmen political bureau on Baghdad Street killing one and injuring three others.

7. Unarmed civilian residents were evicted at gunpoint and many innocent Turkmen and Arabs were killed.

8. The KDP members forced the Turkmen people in many of their local districts to raise KDP flags. One witness named Semih Serdar Sabir later told reporters these civilians were continuously threatened by the Kurds.

9. A local city council of 24 people was formed consisting of Turkmen, Assyrian, Arabs, and Kurds in equal numbers. Despite a Turkmen presence of roughly 70 per cent of Kirkuk's total population, Kurdish governor Abdurrahman Mustafa was appointed without

being elected. This governor employed more than 7,000 Kurds in different government locations throughout the region. Moreover, five more Kurdish members and one Arab were added, dominating the council.

10. The Kurds that occupied Kirkuk proclaimed the city as a part of so-called Kurdistan and underestimated the Turkmen population to a half million all over Iraq. PUK leader Jalal Talabani misrepresented the Turkmen population on several occasions.

11. A large number of private cars were stolen in front of their owners. Many Turkmen were killed when they refused to give up their vehicles.

12. Banks and the central market of Kirkuk were burned after all their contents were removed.

13. The communications and transportation networks of the city were completely destroyed. Electric poles, high-voltage cables, telephone cables and water pipes of some buildings were totally removed. As a result, the city suffered severely after the occupation due to a lack of communication, sanitation and health care systems.

14. Saddam and Jumhuriya general hospitals were looted and patients were forced to leave. All medical instruments were stolen from both hospitals including computers, beds and incubators.

15. The Kurdish parties had encouraged Kurds from Iran and Syria to settle in Kirkuk. They were provided with false identity cards indicating Kirkuk as their place of birth. It had been noted that over 350,000 outsider Kurds were brought into Kirkuk and daily migration is now continuing unabated.

16. In order to wipe out the Turkmen culture in the city, the Kirkuk television station on the main road to Baghdad was occupied by armed peshmergas and broadcasting equipment was stolen, including the Turkmen archives.

17. Kurds began to buy land and properties in and around Kirkuk.

18. Kurdish forces remained the only armed group in Iraq.

19. The Tomb of Bugday Hatun (one of the daughters of the Sultan Tugrul Bey, whose Seljuk Empire ruled Mesopotamia between

1055-1258) in the Citadel of Kirkuk was vandalized along with other Turkmen historical sites.

20. The Kirkuk central library, which contained numerous valuable historical books, was destroyed.

21. The visit of appointed Iraqi Interim Governor Jay Garner to Sulaimaniyah and Erbil, where parades were staged to mark the victory of the U.S. forces and Operation *IRAQI FREEDOM*:

Following the toppling of Saddam Hussein in April 2003 the American government appointed a retired general, Jay Garner, as the head of the Office of Reconstruction and Humanitarian Affairs (ORHA) in Iraq. Jay Garner had a long history with the Kurds in northern Iraq. He immediately visited the cities of Sulaimaniyah and Erbil and declared Kirkuk as a Kurdish city, which disappointed and angered the Turkmen. The Turkmen in Iraq were looking forward to having equal treatment from the Americans, but unfortunately priority was given to the Kurds.

On one occasion while touring in Erbil, Garner was asked about the structure of the administration in Kirkuk. He decisively replied, "The issue of Kirkuk will soon be the task of the new administration. It is not decided yet who will administrate the Kurdish city of Kirkuk." Shortly after his statement, U.S. Ambassador Paul Bremer replaced Jay Garner.

U.S. President George W. Bush tasked Bremer to be his envoy in Iraq and put him in charge of all civilian U.S. personnel in the country. On May 13, 2003, U.S. Secretary of Defense Donald Rumsfeld appointed Bremer as the administrator of the Coalition Provisional Authority (CPA).

American Jay Garner (centre) celebrates the U.S. victory with Kurdish leaders Jalal Talabani (left) and Masood Barzani (right).

22. Most street and the hospital names were changed to Kurdish names.

23. U.S. troops reportedly killed one Turkmen and arrested two others in Kirkuk. On July 11, 2003 Enver Seyyit Terzi, a prominent Turkmen singer, was shot dead by U.S. soldiers when he was returning from prayers. Two other Turkmen (Timur and Nihat) who were with Terzi in the car were detained.

24. On April 12, 2003 Kurds in the township of Tuz Hurmatu killed three prominent Turkmen – lawyer Ercan Sakir Mustafa, Alican Shakir Mustafa, and 30-year-old Yusuf Kemal Chayir. Another Turkmen, Mustafa Suleyman, was seriously wounded.

25. On April 13, 2003 Kurdish peshmergas launched an attack on the Iraqi Turkmen Front office located on Baghdad Street, Kirkuk. One Turkmen youth was killed and his wounded father went missing.

26. The Kurds killed 44-year-old Nazim Shukur Atwan in the township of Dakuk. Atwan was a prominent member of the Iraqi Turkmen National Party.

27. The old family graveyard of brothers Ata and Ihsan Hayrullah, located in the Citadel of Kirkuk, was destroyed. As mentioned earlier,

The family gravesite of Ata and Ihsan Hayrullah was destroyed (below left) and the statue commemorating the actions of Colonel Ata Hayrullah (below right) was vandalized in the Citadel of Kirkuk.

the Kurds had executed the two brothers during the massacre of July 14, 1959.

28. The statue of Col. Ata Hayrullah standing close to Kirkuk bridge was also damaged. The Kurds were trying to remove the evidence related to the July 14th massacre.

29. Many Turkmen children were killed for raising Iraqi and Turkmen Front Flags.

30. Eight Turkmen were killed and 55 were wounded on December 31, 2003 during a peace rally administrated by the Turkmen and Arabs in Kirkuk in protest of the Kurd's federal system to divide Iraq. Many Turkmen Front offices and other Turkmen parties were attacked killing several.

31. Several Turkmen were killed during an August 22, 2003 demonstration protesting the destruction of the Tomb of Mezar Ali (a sacred place for Shiites) by a group of Kurds in Tuz Hurmatu. The next day, more died during a protest near a government building condemning the previous day's action.

32. Turkmen intellectuals were shot at and many leaders were assassinated. Attempts to assassinate the ITF leader were carried out.

33. Many Turkmen graves were destroyed and the tombstones were replaced by Kurdish names. New graves in the Turkmen cemeteries bearing Kurdish names rapidly appeared. Most of the Turkmen graves were destroyed and the tombstones replaced. Also, the epitaphs that were written in Turkmen scripts on the tombstones have been

After April 10, 2003, the tombstones of Turkmen were disfigured and destroyed, with many replaced by others bearing Kurdish names.

disfigured and replaced by Kurdish writings. It is believed that the rationnale for this was to prove the fake existence of the Kurds in the cities of Kirkuk, Erbil and Mosul. The actions by the KDP and PUK remind us of what has happened to Jewish cemeteries in the past.

34. In order to obtain a birth certificate from Kirkuk, Kurdish women were brought from Sulaimaniyah and Erbil to give birth in Kirkuk hospitals. Many ambulances were designated to bring Kurdish pregnant women to these hospitals.

35. The emptied government buildings and the main stadium in Shorija district were allotted to Kurdish families and organizations claiming they had been deported from Kirkuk city.

36. Kurds brought from Sulaimaniyah, Dohuk, Zakho and Erbil replaced Turkmen employees in all government directorates while the former workers were forcibly taken away.

37. Thousands of Kurdish fighters and peshmerga became members of the Iraqi National Guard, and joined police and security forces in Kirkuk, enabling them to control the authority of the city.

38. Attempts to establish a separate Kurdish state – a federal system based on racism and ethnicity – was proposed without a mandate from the people of Iraq.

39. The Iraqi Turkmen Front was deliberately excluded from the

Turkmen in Kirkuk protest against the discrimination they continue to be subjected to after the removal of Saddam Hussein. Exclusion from the Interim Council and omissions in the new constitution are decried.

Iraqi Governing Council. Thousands of Turkmen rallied demanding that their voice be heard.

40. Turkmen teachers and students were forced either to use the Kurdish language or leave the schools.

41. Kurds controlling the high-level positions in the city would not allow the admission of injured Turkmen during the demonstrations to Kirkuk hospital. As well, reporters from Kirkuk Turkmen TV, who entered the hospital to interview the wounded protesters, were detained in a small room inside the hospital and not allowed to speak with the injured. In one instance, the Kurdish police beat Mohammed Samanchi, the director of a human rights group in Kirkuk, when he and a group of Turkmen tried to donate blood.

THE ERA OF DR. IYAD ALLAWI, 2004-2005

Once again it must be stated that the Turkmen people of Iraq strongly believe the time has come for all Iraqis to disregard the remnants of political squabbles instigated by the former regime of Saddam Hussein and instead focus on the future of Iraq. As such, this means that all Iraqis are required to emphasize national unity and reconciliation. Beyond that, it is also required from all to preserve superior relations with all neighboring and foreign countries. However, sadly when it came to Prime Minister Iyad Allawi's cabinet, once again the Turkmen's political rights were violated. Representatives from the ITF were not even consulted and intentionally excluded from Dr. Allawi's cabinet.

1. Turkmen army and police members were excluded from the newly formed Iraqi Police force (IP) and ING forces (Iraqi National Guard). The Kurdish peshmarga were converted into security forces (IP, ING and special security teams) in Kirkuk and other Turkmen regions.

2. Many Turkmen townships and villages were attacked by the ING, which mainly consisted of Kurdish fighters. The township of Telafer was attacked by coalition forces because of false information provided by the ING against the Turkmen in the city. The population of Telafer, which was estimated at more than 400,000, was evacuated

in August 2003 and people were not allowed to return until five days later. Many districts and schools were destroyed and more than 200 people were killed and injured.

3. The government of Iyad Allawi – he was appointed prime minister and granted authority by U.S. Ambassador Paul Bremer to head the Iraqi interim government on June 28, 2004 and replaced on January 30, 2005 by Ibrahim Al-Jafari after Iraq's first election since Saddam's removal – had excluded the Turkmen from decision-making and participating in the government. Only one Turkmen, Rashad Mandan Omer, was appointed as a technology minister in the newly-formed ministry.

4. The Turkmen were the first Iraqi segment to demonstrate against terrorism on August 6, 2003. In Al Andalus Circle in Baghdad more than 10,000 Turkmen marched condemning the violence.

5. The Turkmen were not mentioned as the third essential component beside Arabs and Kurds in the interim Iraqi constitution. The Turkmen language and their legitimate rights were all denied. Thousands of Turkmen demonstrated in front of the interim council building in Baghdad and they chained themselves and abstained from food and drink for three consecutive days demanding their rights. After the protests, they were told that their rights were granted and the demonstration came to an end. However, the interim government denied the Turkmen legitimate rights in the constitution and furthermore, the Kurds (with the assistance of the ING), attacked and ransacked the ITF headquarters in Kirkuk.

6. Not a single Turkmen was appointed as an ambassador in Iraqi embassies and consulates. The Ministry of Iraqi Foreign Affairs was completely dominated by the Kurds.

7. Turkmen faced visible irregularities during the first Iraqi elections of January 30, 2005.

8. The sign carrying the names of Turkmen martyrs placed in Altun Kopru township cemetery was deliberately disfigured. The sign was created in remembrance of the massacre of more than 135 Turkmen by Saddam Hussein's specials forces in the township of Altun Kopru during the uprising of 1991.

IRREGULARITIES IN IRAQ'S FIRST ELECTION

Before the Iraqi elections, the Independent Electoral Commission of Iraq (IECI) was created in Baghdad with sub-commission offices all over the country. Based on information conducted regarding the voters in Kirkuk, the sub-commission had decided that about 459,105 people were eligible to vote in the city elections. The IECI also requested the proof of official papers (i.e. identity card, land registry documents, diplomas from Kirkuk schools and passports). They had determined the Kurds in Kirkuk committed more than 90,000 forgeries, and therefore they were all excluded from the elections. However, U.S. Deputy Secretary of State Richard Armitage's visit to Iraq changed the decision made by the IECI in Kirkuk.

Armitage first met with KDP leader Massoud Barzani and PUK leader Jalal Talabani in the north before meeting with Iraqi President Gazi Al-Yawar and Prime Minister Iyad Allawi. After his visit to the north, orders were issued to the IECI to include the Kurds in the voting lists in Kirkuk. The Kurds then took advantage of the decision and brought thousands of additional Kurds into Kirkuk. Following the new orders issued from the IECI in Baghdad, the sub-commission in Kirkuk had prolonged the period of registration and 17-25 new Kurd-only registration centers were opened. Therefore, it has been estimated that over 108,000 Kurdish voters were unjustly added to the Kirkuk voting list.

RIGHT: *A sign with the names of Turkmen martyrs killed during the 1991 uprising was vandalized.*
FAR RIGHT: *Iraqi police line up to vote.*

Since April 9, 2003, the Turkmen people of Iraq have been deprived of their political, cultural, social and national rights because of the influence of forces trying to disintegrate Iraq. In the face of all these atrocities, they decided to participate in the Iraqi elections to restore democracy and to build a new Iraq where equality and human rights could be preserved. However, despite all the efforts put forward by the Iraqi Turkmen Front to achieve free and fair elections, the Kurds continued to commit widespread irregularities in the Turkmen region. The reason for this is that their intention was to collect more votes to regain control of Kirkuk and prepare for the future referendum to annex the city to the so-called Kurdistan.

Although the Independent Electoral Commission of Iraq declared the election was fair, numerous irregularities and violations were encountered in the Turkmen region. Based on the legal rights granted to political parties and organizations to submit their concerns to the IECI, the Iraqi Turkmen Front managed to collect the following violations that occurred during the election process in the regions of Kirkuk, Erbil, Diyalah, Mosul, Salahaddin and many other areas:

1. Before the Iraqi elections, approximately 300,000 Kurds were allowed to settle in Kirkuk under the belief that they were original inhabitants of the city. The new settlers were Kurds brought by the Patriotic Union of Kurdistan (PUK) and the Democratic Party of

A sign advertising for the Kurdish coalition is prominently displayed on a municipal building in Kirkuk. This is in direct violation of the IECI rules which prohibit the promotion of all political parties on government buildings.

Kurdistan (KDP) from Iran, Syria and northern Iraq. Their intention in bringing the new settlers into Kirkuk was to alter the population distribution of the city and eventually diminish the Turkmen proportion.

2. Before April 2003 Kirkuk's population was approximately 880,000, but after the fall of Saddam this number increased to more than a million. Just before the election, the population climbed to 1,200,000, which strongly indicates an abnormal increase due to the new Kurdish settlers.

3. The chief of the electoral commission in Kirkuk, Yahya Asi Al Hadidi, determined the existence of over 90,000 illegal Kurds who had settled in the city. However, he was then forced to resign due to intolerable pressure and direct threats from KDP and PUK officials. As well, eight other members from the same commission resigned or were dismissed.

4. Before the elections, the Kurds attacked the Iraqi Turkmen Front headquarters and offices and many guards and officials were injured.

5. The Kurds violated the IECI election rules and regulations by hanging Kurdish coalition list posters on the walls of government buildings in Kirkuk and other regions.

6. The Kurds attacked the Iraqi Turkmen Front Cultural Centre in Hay Al Askeri in Kirkuk, but no injuries were reported. The Kurdish militia was attempting to arrest a Turkmen official at the same building.

7. Arabs who lived for centuries in Kirkuk with the Turkmen refused to participate in the election. They boycotted the IECI for allowing more than 100,000 new Kurdish settlers to head to the polls.

8. On Al Jumhuriya Street the Kurdish militia attacked a member of the Iraqi Turkmen Front while he was putting up election posters.

9. Thousands of Turkmen families were denied pre-registration according to the food rationing cards.

10. The Iraqi Turkmen Front logo was intentionally deleted from the candidate names booklet. The Independent Electoral Commission of Iraq collected all distributed booklets and put on a new ITF logo

with different colors (purple and black instead of the original blue and white).

11. The Turkmen language was not permitted at all during the election process on materials such as posters, ballot papers, instructions, and badges. Despite all the efforts made by the ITF to use the Turkmen language, only Arabic and Kurdish were used besides English.

12. Sermet Kerkuklu, a member of the Turkmeneli student and youth organization, was seriously injured after the Kurdish militia attacked him while he was distributing election pamphlets. Kerkuklu was admitted to a hospital for his injuries.

13. Provocative declarations made by both KDP and PUK leaders raised the tension in Kirkuk before the elections. KDP leader Massoud Barzani declared war against the people of Kirkuk. He insisted that Kirkuk was a Kurdish city and they were ready to fight for it. Barzani government Human Rights Minister Dr. Muhammed Ihsan declared the Kirkuk issue a Kurdish issue since he said it belonged to the so-called Kurdistan. Hushyar Zebari, the Kurdish Iraqi interim government foreign minister, declared that the Kirkuk issue is an Iraqi internal issue. Berhum Salih, the Kurdish deputy prime minister during Allawi's government, also declared Kirkuk was a Kurdish city during a visit there.

14. Prominent Turkmen writer Ekrem Tuzlu was attacked upon leaving the Turkmeneli TV where he called people to vote for the Turkmen coalition list 175. He was taken to the hospital with many injuries.

15. Although under the terms of the curfew imposed on Kirkuk cars were not allowed to enter the city, a huge number of Kurds from the provinces of Erbil and Sulaimaniyah were brought into Kirkuk.

16. The Kurds in Raheem Awa district and those brought from Erbil and Sulaimaniyah have voted more then once. It was reported that some voted more than five times in different stations without inking their fingers. These irregularities were committed under the supervision of Kurdish election supervisors.

17. The election supervisors and assessors were all Kurdish in majority Kurdish populated districts such as Raheem Awa, Shorija

and Imam Kasim in contradiction with the election rules and regulations.

18. A considerable number of underage Kurds were permitted to vote in Manjouli School located behind the old Al Karama security building in Raheem Awa. Similar situations occurred in Arafa election centres.

19. Many Kurds used their deceased relative's papers to vote in the election centre at Assiri School located behind the Andalus police station in Raheem Awa district. In one instance, a Kurdish voter named Hussain Saber voted on behalf of his father Saber Abu Al Dajaj who had died several years earlier.

20. About 3,000 Kurdish members of the Iraqi National Guard were allowed to vote more than once. The ING were allowed to vote once at the election centre close to their duty place and a second time at the election centres of their residency places.

21. In the city of Erbil, where over 350,000 Turkmen live, tens of thousands of these voters were forced to use lead pencils instead of ballpoint pens or markers to cast their vote. Thousands of Turkmen votes were accredited to the Kurdish coalition list 130 without the presence of international and non-Kurdish observers.

22. Many Turkmen in Erbil were forced to vote for the Kurdish coalition list 130 after receiving direct threats from the KDP.

23. The Kurds who refused to vote for the Kurdish coalition list 130 in Erbil, Sulaimaniyah, and Dahouk were pronounced traitors by the PUK and KDP.

24. Despite the absence of the Arab inhabitants from the elections in the two villages of Maftul Al Saghir and Maftul Al Kabir of Tuz Hurmatu region, it has been announced that the inhabitants of these two villages have voted 100 per cent for Kurdish coalition list 130.

25. Although the official closing time for polling stations was deemed to be 5 p.m., the voting process in the Kurdish-dominated regions in Kirkuk and Tuz Hurmatu continued until late hours. The observers from the non-Kurdish parties who objected to the irregularities were badly treated and insulted by the members of the National Guard. Many observers were expelled from the election

centres at gunpoint.

26. The Kurds in the Iraqi National Guard manipulated the election results after taking control of the election centres in Sulayman Beg, a town in the Tuz Hurmatu region, where the inhabitants are Turkmen and Arabs. It was found that all the votes of this town supported the Kurdish coalition list 130.

27. Eight new spontaneous voting centres were opened in Kirkuk on the day of the election without the consent of the Election Commission in Kirkuk. More than 3,000 heavily armed peshmergas from Sulaimaniyah province were brought into Kirkuk in order to guard these improvised stations.

28. The police in Kirkuk, whose members are from different ethnic groups, were prevented from performing their duties during the day of the election. They were stopped from approaching improvised voting centres. The following are the names of schools (voting centres) that were not issued by the Election Commission in Kirkuk:

    A) Goran School

    B) Alaa School

    C) Imam Qasim Industrial School

    D) Mamosta Rashad Martyr School

    E) Mahabad School

    F) Imam Qasim School

    G) Iskan School

    H) 11th of April School

29. Insufficient ballot papers in many election centres in the Turkmen region, especially Kirkuk, prevented some members of this community from voting. This matter caused many Turkmen voting centres in Kirkuk and other areas to close before 5 p.m. It has been declared that ballot papers were stolen by the ING, which was the only force allowed at night in Kirkuk and its surrounding regions. This effectively occurred in the Atabegler School election centre in "The 1st March" district of Kirkuk.

30. The locations of some of the election centres in the Turkmen districts of Kirkuk were moved to Kurdish districts one day before

the election. These centres were relocated to predominantly Kurdish districts in order to prevent Turkmen voters from travelling to these regions. For instance, the location of Al Wakeel Muhammed Ali Sadiq election centre, which was supposed to be installed in Marrakesh School, was moved to Assiri School in a Kurdish area.

31. In the election centres in Raheem Awa, the majority of Kurdish inhabitants opened at 6 a.m. (one hour earlier than the official opening time) in order to aid the Kurds who were brought to Kirkuk from Sulaimaniyah and Erbil to vote. This action was well organized by the PUK and KDP in order to increase the Kurdish vote in Kirkuk.

32. Two ballot boxes from the Abi Tammam election centre were stolen. Much suspicion arose that this was by the ING Kurdish forces.

33. The intrusion of many Kurdish groups associated with the Kurdish organizations in several election centres caused intimidation and disorder. The Kurdish associations known as "Komala 63 Kirkuk" intimidated the Turkmen voters. They distributed pamphlets and used physical threats to prevent the Turkmen from voting. Beyond that this group was accused of manipulating the ballot counting in Arafa district.

34. The insufficient number of election centres in the city of Telafer prevented a large number of Turkmen electors from voting. Only two election centres were opened in a city with a population of over 400,000 Turkmen. The distance between the election centres and voter's residences, military operations, bombings in the city during election day, and the use force by the ING all discouraged and stopped thousands of voters.

35. The absence of ballot boxes from the towns of Aliyadhiya and Muhallabiyya and the villages surrounding them in the Telafer region prevented at least 20,000 Turkmen to participate in the elections.

36. The ballot boxes stolen in the town of Mansuriyyah prevented another 3,000 from voting. Many believe the ING is to be blamed for the incident.

37. The polling centre in the Turkmen village of Bir Ahmet was ordered to open at 10 a.m. by the peshmerga groups and was closed

earlier at 3.30 p.m. The Kurdish militia took the ballot boxes to an unknown location under the guise that the American forces required the boxes. The next day these boxes were returned to the Election Commission after they were accredited for the Kurdish coalition list 130.

38. Through the use of threats and intimidations, the Kurds forcibly dominated the election process in the Turkmen regions. The electoral commission employed hundreds of Kurds, while most of the Turkmen were excluded. Although a small number of Turkmen were selected to work for this election, many employees and observers were forced out of the centres before the closing and sealing of the ballot boxes.

39. Full collaboration was noticed between the PUK and KDP officials and the election employees and observers in most centres in the Kurdish districts. Many argue that these ties between the two resulted in numerous fraudulent results and irregularities.

40. Despite the total ban imposed on all vehicles across the country, the Kurds were allowed to move throughout their districts, particularly in Raheem Awa, where they exhibited Kurdish flags, sung their national anthem and shouted provocative propaganda slogans against the Turkmen in Kirkuk. The ING force was kept silent over the intimidations.

41. The election employees in Raheem Awa prevented Kurds from choosing anything other than Kurdish lists, pretending that the Kurdish law forbade them from voting for a non-Kurdish list.

42. In addition to official lists that were distributed to all voters according to the food rationing cards or food stamps, the Kurds also used non-official ballot papers. This was observed in several election centres in the Kurdish region in Kirkuk. For example, in the Wasiti election centre it was found that many unofficial stamped papers were used extensively. Food rationing cards were established by the former regime during UN economic sanctions.

43. The Kurdish voters were provided with multiple ballot papers in several election stations in their districts. However, the non-Kurdish election observers in these centres were prevented from reporting

the action.

44. Turkmeneli TV cameraman Abdullah Ziyaeldin was taken into custody while he was filming some irregularities in the Raheem Awa election centres. His camera was destroyed and he was physically abused by the peshmergas.

45. Despite the ban imposed in Kirkuk on circulating between towns and localities on the day of the election, the roads between Kirkuk, Erbil and Sulaimaniyah remained open. This resulted in tens of thousands of Kurds flowing into the city without any restrictions, allowing them to vote more than once. The transportation of the Kurds from Sulaimaniyah and Erbil into Kirkuk was obviously organized under the supervision of the chief of the Iraqi Police in Kirkuk General Shirko Shakir, as well as the Kurdish ING Commander, General Anwar.

The local branch of the PUK supervised this influx and accommodated the new settlers in the schools of Raheem Awa and in numerous private Kurdish family homes. Not only were these individuals allowed to register and vote in Kirkuk, they were also permitted to register and vote in Erbil and Sulaimaniyah as well.

46. One hundred and fifty official election badges were designated for the vehicles of officials in the province of Kirkuk. However 50 badges were handed over by Ismail Al Hadidi, the deputy governor of Kirkuk, to the Kurdish director of the Election Commission in Kirkuk. The remaining badges and circulation permits were then given to individuals circulating in vehicles belonging to the security department of Sulaimaniyah province (known as the Asaish). Ismail Al Hadidi is known for his affiliation with the Kurdish parties. He was a candidate in the Kurdish coalition list 130.

47. The Kurdish ING forces in the election process in Kirkuk and Leylan prevented Turkmen electors. Although it is assumed that the duty of the police is to serve, protect and to act neutrally, the Kurdish members of the Iraqi Police and ING forces always acted for the Kurds.

48. In the Turkmen towns of Yengija and Bastamli, Kurdish militia members collected the ballot boxes and transferred them to

an unknown location. In Yengija alone, 18 ballot boxes were taken and one box was found dropped on the street with all the papers dispersed. The transferred boxes were later brought back to the Election Commission with the results suspiciously supporting the Kurds.

49. A Kurdish officer from the security department of Sulaimaniyah (Asaish) known as "Kak Tariq" was appointed as deputy director of the election commission in Tuz Hurmatu the day of the election. His last-minute nomination influenced and caused numerous irregularities during the elections.

50. Members from the Kurdish Asaish security forces attacked Mumtaz Ahmad, the director of the election centre of Ibn Khaldoon where he was detained. The Asaish had stolen many ballot boxes and returned them the next day with one missing. This will also indicate with little doubt that the ballot papers were all manipulated and modified for the Kurdish coalition list 130.

51. According to many Turkmen sources, the Kurds used several tactics to intimidate voters. These included irregularities, physical assault and aggression against election officials, illegal segregation, manipulation of ballot papers, and confiscation of ballot boxes.

52. The voter lists that were not used for the Kurdish coalition list 130 were destroyed in Erbil, Kirkuk, Mosul and Diyalah.

53. The Kurdish ING forces raided three polling stations in Musalla and Tisin and the ballot boxes were taken to an unknown location.

54. Turkmen and Arab candidates went missing from the election lists in many areas in Kirkuk such as Hay I Adar, Tareek, Baghdad and Tisin.

55. The Kurdish militia, who were carrying election badges written in their language, would try to intimidate the Turkmen as they approached their voting centres.

56. Mrs. Labiba Kerkukly, a prominent Turkmen woman and candidate in the Iraqi Turkmen Front coalition list, was seriously beaten by the Kurdish militia in a Kirkuk private secondary school in Arafa. The Kurdish militia took the ballot boxes to an unknown location after deleting the Turkmen Front coalition name from the

election list.

57. According to the Al-Watan information centre in Iraq, the following irregularities were counted after conducting interviews with observers:

A) Ali Aydin Jalil, an observer in the Abi Tammam Altai School election centre, reported that two ballot boxes were stolen from the same location at night. Also, a group of Kurdish militia had put some extra ballot boxes outside the same station for the Kurds with the hope they would vote to determine the future of Kirkuk and eventually annex it to so-called Kurdistan.

B) According to Mrs. Guler Baker Hassan, an observer in Alsadir High School election centre, the ING Kurdish militia voted twice. In one incident, a fight broke out between one of the observers and the Kurdish presiding officer in the centre after the individual tried to stop the militia from voting more than once.

C) According to Nihat Baker Amin, an observer in Al Musalla High School election station in Musalla district, there were numerous irregularities on ballot boxes No. 31912 and 31907 for the municipal election and boxes No. 31309 and 31906 for general elections. It was reported that Ali Amin Wali, a Kurdish instructor in the same election centre station, was providing the Kurds with several ballot papers to vote more than once.

D) The Kurdish officials from outside of Kirkuk were in charge of organizing the elections and instructing the Kurds how to vote more than once.

E) Imad Muhammed Samin, an observer in election centre-381, reported that ballot boxes No.39934, 39933, 39932, and 39931 from Mohammed Alsadik election centre were all transferred to an unknown location.

F) Hussien Abbas Hamid Beg, an observer in Mohammed Alsadik election centre, had detected numerous irregularities in ballot boxes designated for general elections No.144575,

144576, 144577, 144578, and 144579 and ballot boxes for municipal elections No.144571, 144572, 144573, 14457 under seal number 14458. He also indicated that groups from different Kurdish political parties had entered the station with no permission from the electoral commission directing people to vote for the Kurdish coalition list 130. It should be noted that the election regulations do not permit propaganda activities inside polling stations.

G) Najat Saed Zaynal, an observer in Menjue election centre located at the back of Al Karama security building, said the Turkmen registrars and observers were expelled from the polling station after 5 p.m. and only the Kurds remained to count the ballots.

H) Nejdet Mardan Mustafa, an observer in Izdihar High School election centre, had detected irregularities in ballot box No. 40440 designated for the general elections. He also noted that the Kurdish militia was distributing $50 US for people voting for Kurdish coalition list 130 in front of the election centres where they set up private tents. Mr. N. Mardan indicated also that five extra Kurds were employed in the same election centre without the permission of the Iraqi election committee.

I) Faruk Aswad Muhyaddin, an observer from Zubeyir Bin Awwam School election centre, indicated that Kurdish observers allowed the Kurds to use illegal papers in voting.

J) Omar Taher Mohammed, an observer in Mohammed Sadek Female Elementary School, had detected the following irregularities in ballot boxes No. 0173256, 0173257 and 0173258:

i) The Kurdish groups holding green and yellow badges were forcing people to vote for the Kurdish coalition list 130.

ii) At 10 p.m. Omar Taher had noticed the presence of the same Kurdish green and yellow badge-holders in the election centre after forcing the non-Kurdish registrars and observers to leave the station at 5 p.m. Green badge holders were representing the PUK and yellow were representing the KDP.

iii) The Kurdish voters could vote for those who could not attend, but still had their names on the lists.

iv) Many Kurds voted more than once for Kurdish coalition list 130 despite having voting ink on their index finger.

58. In Al Hawija town where the majority are Arabs, only several ballot boxes in the capacity of 20,000 voters were sent and 60,000 voters were deprived from voting. The Kurds anticipated that the Arabs in Al Hawija might vote for the Turkmen.

59. Adequate ballot papers were not sent to the Turkmen regions.

60. Many ballot boxes were taken into the Kurdish tent camp in Kenar district in Kirkuk and thousands of votes were illegally added. The *Zaman Turkish* newspaper correspondent Kursat Bayhan in Kirkuk detected this situation on February 2, 2005 while interviewing some Kurds at the same camp. Kurds also informed the correspondent that they were not originally from Kirkuk. They were brought from Baghdad, Sulaimaniyah, Erbil and Iran.

61. Turkmen in Erbil city were prevented from performing promotional activities for the Iraqi Turkmen Front coalition list 175. Many Turkmen posters were damaged and destroyed by Kurdish militia forces.

62. Unusual increase in the population of the following regions were noticed due to the participation of the Kurds from Erbil and Sulaimaniyah in the elections:

Name of Region	Original Pop.	During Elections
Township of Altun Kopru	11,560	17,711
Township of Shiwan	2,442	9,566
Township of Kara Incir	3,382	11,206
Azadi district (Kirkuk)	23,200	90,648
Rahimawa district (Kirkuk)	20,000	76,149

It was estimated that at least 84,000 outsider Kurds participated in the elections in Kirkuk in the regions mentioned above.

63. Only Kurds were allowed to enter the ballot counting centre located in the food depot centre in Hay Al Wasiti while Turkmen and Arabs were excluded.

64. The absence of the international observers in Kirkuk resulted in numerous forgeries.

65. The Independent Electoral Commission of Iraq admitted the irregularities conducted in several Iraqi provinces through press releases and media announcements. According to IECI spokesperson Farid Ayar, irregularities were detected in Kirkuk and Mosul. He blamed some armed groups for changing the ballot boxes by force and bribes.

66. Saip Zaman, a Turkmen major in Leylan, was detained for eight days by the ING when he tried to prevent peshmergas from manipulating the elections.

67. Under the supervision of the PUK and KDP, members of the Kurdish Workers' Party (known as the PKK, they are an extremist Kurdish separatist group based out of Turkey) also participated in the Iraqi elections. Posters of captured PKK leader Abdullah Ocalan (captured in Turkey, many of his party members fled into northern Iraq) were posted in many districts in Kirkuk. Thousands of Kurds from Turkey settled in Kirkuk as part of the Kurdish project to change the Turkmen identity of the city.

THE ERA OF IBRAHIM AL-JAFARI, 2005–

To preserve the Turkmen's rights in Iraq, the Iraqi Turkmen Front entered the Iraqi elections of January 30, 2005 as an individual list under number-175. After the irregularities and fraudulent activities carried out against the Turkmen, the ITF gained only three seats in the Iraqi National Assembly. The Islamic Union of Iraqi Turkmen allied with the Shiites in coalition list-169 supported by the Shiite clerk El Sistani gained only four seats in the Iraqi National Assembly. The Islamic Union of Iraqi Turkmen was granted a minister in Dr. Ibrahim Al-Jafari's cabinet, but the Kurdish parties imposed a veto to exclude the ITF from the interim government. It was decided that the fourth deputy prime minister was designated to the Turkmen, but this seat has remained unoccupied. For the same results, the Kurds have gained 21 seats in the city council of Kirkuk while the Turkmen gained nine and the Arabs six.

CREATING A NEW CONSTITUTION FOR IRAQ

It can be said with great certainty, that for the past three decades the Turkmen suffered the most in Iraq. Saddam Hussein had an unusual hatred against the Turkmen who had established more than six dynasties and states in Iraq throughout the country's history. Oil and the strategic location of Turkmen settlements were the main cause of their suffering.

Turkmen dwellings and villages were totally destroyed and their residents were force to migrate. Hundreds of Turkmen leaders and intellectuals were executed and many thousands went missing. In order to change the Turkmen identity of their regions and particularly in Kirkuk, a harsh Arabification policy was applied. Thousands of Turkmen were displaced and thousands more were forced to leave the country. In their place scores of Arabs settled in Kirkuk. Speaking in Turkmen language was prohibited. Turkmen cultivated lands were expropriated. The township of Tisin located to the south of Kirkuk was bulldozed and more than 20,000 Turkmen were displaced. More than 500 Turkmen in Tisin were martyred and many others went missing. The Arabification policy was designed to wipe out the Turkmen population in Kirkuk and its vicinities. The Turkmen were forced to change their ethnicity during October 10, 1987 census by registering either as Arab or Kurd. Several massacres in 1991, 1996, 1998 and 2000 were applied against the Turkmen during the former regime of Iraq.

During the 1991 uprising, the Kurdish peshmergas had destroyed the city's Land Registry and Population Registry Offices, an action that was again repeated in April 2003. In 1996, the KDP leader Massoud Barzani had invited the Iraqi army to enter the city of Erbil to eliminate the PUK influence. However, only the Turkmen were attacked while the PUK forces swiftly fled the city. More than 300 Turkmen were killed in the township of Altun Kopru and their bodies were recently found in the mass graves near Dibis. Many Turkmen mass graves were also found in Sari Tepe and near Dakuk. During the 1996 massacre many Turkmen political offices in Erbil were destroyed and 17 Turkmen politicians were executed on the spot and more than 100 were taken to different Iraqi prisons. Despite all the atrocities applied against the Turkmen, their loyalty to Iraq has remained unchanged.

The Turkmen people of Iraq do not believe in fighting and they always demanded their rights through the use of civilized methods. They were never involved in an armed struggle against the previous Iraqi governments. Overall, it can be argued that the Turkmen are the most educated people in Iraq. It has been reported that between 85 to 90 per cent of the total population have at least a high school diploma.

The Turkmen had played a great role in history in mediating between the Arabs and the Kurds. As a result, for stability to occur in Iraq, the Turkmen must be involved.

Despite all of these factors about the Turkmen, they were excluded from the political field in Iraq. The Turkmen were shocked when their rights were totally ignored in the Interim Iraqi Constitution. However they demanded their rights in a civil way. Turkmen demonstrations took place in Baghdad and Kirkuk calling for their legitimate rights, but because of powerful political parties they were denied. Turkmen representatives were both excluded from the Iraqi Interim Council and the interim government. Finally, the Turkmen were not fairly represented in the constitution committee and as a result their voices were not heard in the blueprint for the future of Iraq.

CONCERNS ON THE CONSTITUTION

The Turkmen people of Iraq have waited patiently to see their legitimate rights in the new draft constitution, but unfortunately more injustices and unfairness has been applied against them. They were stunned by the limited rights stated in the draft constitution. Moreover they were deprived of basic human, political, social, cultural and economical rights.

It has been estimated that the Turkmen constitute around 13 per cent of the total population of Iraq, but higher percentages have also been proposed. As mentioned earlier, the Turkmen are the third largest ethnic group in Iraq after the Arabs and the Kurds and their number is estimated at around three million people.

The Iraqi Turkmen Front has reviewed the new draft constitution cautiously, and forwarded the Turkmen's concerns to the Iraqi National Assembly for consideration, but unfortunately the application has remained unanswered.

The Turkmen were unfairly treated in the new draft constitution including the Preface and particularly in Articles 2,4,23,108,115,122, 136 and 138.

PREFACE

The Turkmen people of Iraq were very happy to see the word "Turkmen" after the Arabs and the Kurds in the preface of the draft constitution indicating that they are the third largest ethnic group in Iraq. It stated that, "Remembering the pains of the despotic band's sectarian oppression of the majority; inspired by the suffering of Iraq's martyrs – Sunni and Shiite, Arab, Kurd and Turkmen, and the remaining brethren in all communities." Unfortunately, the happiness ended very soon when the Turkmen were listed among the others and their language was not stated as the third official language in Iraq.

When describing the oppressions committed against all Iraqi segments by the former regime of Saddam Hussein, it stated that, "… inspired by the injustice against the holy cities in the popular uprising and against the marshes and other places; recalling the agonies of the national oppression in the massacres of Halabja, Barzan, Anfal and against the Faili Kurds; inspired by the tragedies of the Turkmen in Beshir and the suffering of the people of the western region."

The fact that the agonies of some Iraqi segments were stated as "national oppression," while the ordeal and aggressions committed against the Turkmen who had suffered the most were stated only as "tragedy" is a tragedy in itself. Indeed Beshir, a small village located to the south of Kirkuk, was bulldozed and the Turkmen residents were displaced, but what about the incidents against the Turkmen in Kirkuk? The Arabification policy? The bulldozing of Tisin and Hamzeil? The displacement of Turkmen citizens and attacks on their languages and culture? The destruction of cultural artifacts such as the Citadel of Kirkuk? And finally, the massacres of hundreds across Turkmen regions?

In another paragraph in the preface it is stated that, "we can create a new Iraq, Iraq of the future, without sectarianism, racial strife, regionalism, discrimination or isolation." But one can clearly see that the words "sectarianism," "racial strife," "regionalism," "discrimination" and "isolation" were all applied only against the Turkmen since April 2003.

Beyond the fact that all Turkmen agonies and suffering were not respectably stated in the draft, several techniques were used to hide the Turkmen identity of Kirkuk, Erbil and many other regions.

ARTICLE-1

> *"The Republic of Iraq is an independent, sovereign nation, and the system of rule in it is a democratic, federal, representative (parliamentary) republic."*

Throughout history Iraq was one united country embracing different ethnic groups (Arabs, Kurds, Turkmen, Assyrians, Armenians and many other small groups and beliefs). Therefore, the term federal would not apply to Iraq because a federation (from the Latin *foedus*, meaning covenant) is a state comprised of a number of self-governing regions (often themselves referred to as "states") united by a central "federal" government. In a federation, the self-governing status of the component states is constitutionally entrenched and may not be altered by a unilateral decision of the central government.

The Iraqi Turkmen Front had participated in all former opposition meetings and always stood against the proposals intended to divide the country. The proposed federal system in Iraq eventually will divide Iraq into north and south or many other regions and consequently will divide the Turkmen land and nation among the proposed regions. As such, we oppose a federal system based on ethnic and geographical distribution. In fact, any federal system based on these factors will create ethnic problems and allow the fortified groups to dominate the region and overrule the other segments. Diversity is the symbol of Iraq; therefore, any system based on ethnicity will result in dividing the country into small regions.

To determine the type of administrative system, Iraqis should hold a general referendum. However, the federal system has been proposed and implemented in the draft without the consent of the Iraqi people. Instead, we recommend an administrative federal system. This system will preserve land and national unity. The local councils or governments would be the principal authority in the provinces and will perform the duties. The councils should be elected democratically, and in order to represent the province's ethnical components, consensus should be taken in consideration. All local councils should be obligated to the central government in Baghdad.

For a comparative example of this type of administrative structure, we recommend taking a look at the system in Canada. The federal system in Canada is an outstanding example of how three separate governments can exist – federal, provincial and municipal or local – and yet work together with one another.

Generally, the federal government takes responsibility for things that affect all citizens. This would include national defence and security, foreign policy and citizenship, revenue, customs and border services.

Provincial governments look after things like education, health and highways and other things that apply to a province specifically. Municipal or local governments in each city or community, meanwhile, are responsible for areas that are directly related to a city such as policing, firefighting and many other municipal works.

Looking back to Iraq, a federal system based on ethnicity and geographical distribution is strongly rejected because it would assimilate the Turkmen nation. If the administrative federal system was disregarded and the system described in the draft was implemented then the Turkmen would have no choice but to insist on establishing the Turkmeneli Federation to protect their own legitimate land and rights.

ARTICLE-2

"1 (c) No law can be passed that contradicts the rights and basic freedoms outlined in this constitution."

This is a clear indication that whatever limited rights were offered to the Turkmen would remain unchanged.

ARTICLE-4

"1st – Arabic and Kurdish are the two official languages for Iraq. Iraqis are guaranteed the right to educate their children in their mother tongues, such as Turkmen or Assyrian, in government educational institutions, or any other language in private educational institutions, according to educational regulations.

"2nd – the scope of the phrase "official language" and the manner of implementing the rules of this article will be defined by a law that includes:

(a) Issuing the official gazette in both languages.

(b) Speaking, addressing and expressing in official domains, like the parliament, Cabinet, courts and official conferences, in either of the two languages.

(c) Recognition of official documents and correspondences in the two languages and the issuing of official documents in them both.

(d) The opening of schools in the two languages in accordance with educational rules.

(e) Any other realms that require the principle of equality, such as currency bills, passports, stamps.

"3rd – Federal agencies and institutions in the region of Kurdistan use both languages.

"4th – The Turkmen and Assyrian languages will be official in the areas where they are located.

"5th – Any region or province can take a local language as an ad-

ditional official language if a majority of the population approves in a universal referendum."

The main object of Article-4 is to affirm that both Arabic and Kurdish are the official languages in Iraq, a statement that totally disregards the Turkmen language. As a matter of fact, slight differences will appear when comparing between the Turkmen and the Kurdish population. The Turkmen constitute 13 per cent of the total population while the Kurds are between 14 to 16 per cent at most. However, the Turkmen do not object to the use of both languages, but are asking for their language to be declared the third official language. For example in Switzerland, despite the fact that only one per cent of citizens actually speaks the old Roman language, it is still considered to be one of the official languages. This example raises many questions when 13 per cent of Iraqis speak Turkmen.

When recalling previous Iraqi constitutions, Article-17 of the Iraqi constitution of March 21, 1925 stated, "Arabic shall be the official language, except as may be prescribed by special law." Article 6, of the same constitution stated, "There shall be no differentiation in the rights of Iraqis before the law, whatever differences may exist in language, race or creed." This could be translated to mean, "the rights of all Iraqis are guaranteed without discrimination." Moreover, Iraq entered into an agreement when they joined the League of Nations in October 3, 1932 that obligated them to respect the human, cultural, and administration rights of the Turkmen and other minorities.

The Iraqi constitution amended in 1932 stated the right to teach the Turkmen language in Kirkuk, Kifri, Erbil and Kara Tepe and also in many other Turkmen areas. Unfortunately the Turkmen's fundamental human rights in culture and education were violated by the closure of the Turkmen schools in 1933-1937. The government of Yasin El-Hashimi had totally banned Turkmen studies in 1936. Although in the past decades Iraqi governments gave some rights to the Turkmen, they were not put into practice.

Article-4 paragraph-5 of the draft constitution stated, "any region or province can take a local language as an additional official language if a majority of the population approves in a universal referendum." This can only mean one thing: As the Kurdish settlers continue to pour into Kirkuk eventually they will become the majority and Kurdish will become the official language of the province.

Another example that has been presented regarding the Turkmen and their rights in Iraq was by the briefing of Special Adviser to the UN Secretary-General Lakdhar Brahimi to the Security Council on the political transition process in Iraq. Brahimi stated that, "We believe that the National Conference should be convened on basis of any quota system, though care should be taken to reflect the diversity of country. In this connection, I feel I must convey the justified demand of the Turkmen to be recognized as third largest community in Iraq. Similar demands have been made formulated by other smaller communities. I believe these legitimate demands should be headed, and can be accommodated in the forthcoming constitution."

ARTICLE-9

    "1st – (a) The Iraqi armed forces and security apparatuses consist of the components of the Iraqi people, keeping in consideration their balance and representation without discrimination or exclusion. They fall under the command of the civil authority, defend Iraq, don't act as a tool of oppression of the Iraqi people, don't intervene in political affairs and they play no role in the rotation of power.

    "(b) Forming military militias outside the framework of the armed forces is banned."

The first two paragraphs of Article-9 have been completely violated in Kirkuk and other Turkmen regions. The Iraqi armed forces and security apparatuses consist mainly of Kurds and Arabs and the Turkmen were totally excluded. Keeping the components of the Iraqi people in balance was obviously unbalanced and the Turkmen were clearly discriminated.

The political parties' peshmerga were used against the Turkmen particularly in Kirkuk, Erbil, Telafer and many other Turkmen regions. Hundreds of Turkmen were detained by the PUK and KDP

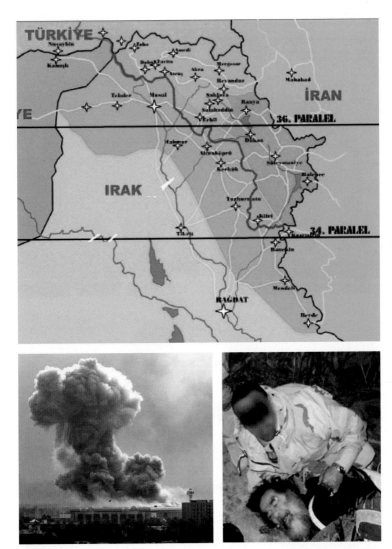

TOP: *A map showing the no-fly zone enforced by the United States and British air forces prior to the second Gulf War. The blue section indicates Turkmen settlements.* ***ABOVE LEFT:*** *In March 2003, the U.S. began its attack on Iraq.* ***ABOVE RIGHT:*** *Saddam Hussein's reign came to an end when, after eight months in hiding, he was captured.* (GETTY IMAGES)

TOP: *Following Saddam Hussein's removal from power, Kurdish fighters were seen destroying and looting government offices.* **ABOVE:** *Masked Kurdish members of the Iraqi National Guard pictured during the attack on Telafer in September 2004.*

CLOCKWISE FROM TOP LEFT: *A Turkmen woman chained herself in protest after a Turkmen director of the ministry of Education was removed from power and replaced by a Kurd. U.S. soldiers removed Turkmen protesting in Baghdad in 2003 after the Iraqi National Council, created by Paul Bremer, did not appoint a single ITF member. A Turkmen boy holds a sign indicating that if one dies, 1,000 will be resurrected. A Turkmen and his children at a voting station in Holland.*

LEFT: A portrait of Zehra Bektas, who set herself on fire protesting the atrocities committed against the Turkmen in the city of Kirkuk in 1959. She is remembered as a Turkmen martyr.
BELOW: The Muhammediye Mosque was destroyed in the fighting.

The Bugday Hatun Tomb in the Citadel of Kirkuk was vandalized on April 10, 2003.

Turkmen men and women residing in Canada (pictured above) (and in other countries) protested the proposed Iraqi constitution. Rallies were also held in Baghdad (opposite top) and Kirkuk (middle and bottom).

TOP: *Turkmen gathered in Kirkuk to protest the federal system being imposed by the Kurds in an effort to separate the north from the south.*
ABOVE: *A man holds a sign stating "Without Turkmen there is no Kirkuk."*

forces in Kirkuk and sent to unknown prisons in northern Iraq. These militias were used to oppress the unarmed Turkmen and were also used in favor of the Kurdish parties during the Iraqi election of January 30, 2005. Despite paragraph (b) in the same article stating that forming military militias outside the framework of the armed forces is banned, the peshmergas along with other militias remained in tact and were given special status.

ARTICLE-18
"5th – Iraqi citizenship may not be granted for the purposes of a policy of population settlement disrupting the demographic makeup in Iraq."

Thousands of Kurds were brought into Kirkuk and Diyalah from the northern cities of Iraq and neighboring countries. Over 350,000 Kurds were brought from Iran and more than 20,000 from Turkey as well as Syria. They were all provided with forged Iraqi nationality cards indicating Kirkuk as a place of birth.

ARTICLE-21
"2nd – Political asylum to Iraq shall be regulated by law and the political refugee shall not be turned over to a foreign body or force-fully returned to the country from which he has fled.
"3rd – Political asylum shall not be granted to those accused of committing international or terror crimes or to anyone who has caused Iraq harm."

This article will guarantee and secure the presence of the Kurdistan Workers' Party (PKK) in Kirkuk. More than 10,000 PKK members and families were brought into Kirkuk from the former Makhmour Camp by the Kurdish parties. The PKK in Kirkuk and nearby vicinities are in charge of patrolling the city entry checkpoints. Many Turkmen were taken by the PKK to unknown prisons. Despite the fact the PKK was classified as a terrorist organization by U.S.A., they are presently acting in Kirkuk under different names and organizations. For example, the PKK had changed its name to the Kurdistan Freedom and Democracy Congress (KADEK).

ARTICLE-23

> "1st – *Private property is protected and the owner has the right to use it, exploit it and benefit from it within the boundaries of the law.*
>
> "2nd – *Property may not be taken away except for the public interest in exchange for fair compensation. This shall be regulated by law.*
>
> "3rd – *(a) An Iraqi has the right to ownership anywhere in Iraq and no one else has the right to own real estate except what is exempted by law.*
>
> *(b) Ownership with the purpose of demographic changes is forbidden."*

In fact, large-scale violations in Kirkuk have occurred since April 2003. Turkmen lands and properties that were forcibly taken from the Turkmen by the former Iraqi regime during the Arabification scheme were distributed to the new Kurdish settlers.

It has been recorded that since April 9, 2003 more than 350,000 Kurds have entered Kirkuk from the northern provinces of Iraq (Sulaimaniyah, Erbil and Dohuk) as well as from Iran and Syria. The Kurdish migration to Kirkuk is unstoppable. When the Turkmen demanded to repossess their confiscated land and properties, it was strongly rejected by Kirkuk Kurdish Governor Abdurrahman Mustafa.

Therefore, the Turkmen strongly believe that Article 23-b has been completely violated in Kirkuk.

ARTICLE-35

> "1st – *(a) the freedom and dignity of a person are protected.*
>
> *(b) No one may be detained or investigated unless by judicial decision.*
>
> *(c) All forms of torture, mental or physical, and inhuman treatment*

are forbidden. There is no recognition of any confession extracted by force or threats or torture, and the injured party may seek compensation for any physical or mental injury that is inflicted.

"2nd – The state is committed to protecting the individual from coercion in thought, religion or politics, and no one may be imprisoned on these bases."

This was confirmed by the article "Kurdish Officials Sanction Abductions in Kirkuk – U.S. Memo Says Arabs, Turkmen Secretly Sent to the North" posted on the front-page of the *Washington Post* by Steve Fainaru and Anthony Shadid on Wednesday, June 15, 2005. The first paragraphs of the article read:

"Police and security units, forces led by Kurdish political parties and backed by the U.S. military, have abducted hundreds of minority Arabs and Turkmen in this intensely volatile city and spirited them to prisons in Kurdish-held northern Iraq, according to U.S. and Iraqi officials, government documents and families of the victims. Seized off the streets of Kirkuk or in joint U.S.-Iraqi raids, the men have been transferred secretly and in violation of Iraqi law to prisons in the Kurdish cities of Erbil and Sulaimaniyah, sometimes with the knowledge of U.S. forces. The detainees, including merchants, members of tribal families and soldiers, have often remained missing for months; some have been tortured, according to released prisoners and the Kirkuk police chief.

"A confidential State Department cable, obtained by the *Washington Post* and addressed to the White House, Pentagon and U.S. Embassy in Baghdad, said the 'extra-judicial detentions' were part of a 'concerted and widespread initiative' by Kurdish political parties 'to exercise authority in Kirkuk in an increasingly provocative manner.'

"The abductions have 'greatly exacerbated tensions along purely ethnic lines' and endangered U.S. credibility, the nine-page cable, dated June 5, stated. 'Turkmen in Kirkuk tell us they perceive a U.S. tolerance for the practice while Arabs in Kirkuk believe Coalition Forces are directly responsible.'

"Some abduction occurred more than a year ago. But according to

U.S. officials, Kirkuk police and Arab leaders, the campaign surged after the Jan. 30 elections consolidated the two main Kurdish parties' control over the Kirkuk provincial government. The two parties are the Patriotic Union of Kurdistan and the Kurdistan Democratic Party. The U.S. military said it had logged 180 cases; Arab and Turkmen politicians put the number at more than 600 and said many families feared retribution for coming forward."

As a conclusion, the freedom and dignity of the Turkmen in their regions were violated. Hundreds of Turkmen were detained and investigated without judicial decision. Moreover, the Turkmen detainees were mentally and physically tortured. The Turkmen are very concerned about their future in Iraq. The draft constitution will permit the Kurds to overrule and dominate. Consequently, instability, hatred and more bloodshed will continue to occur in the region.

ARTICLE-108

"Oil and gas is the property of all the Iraqi people in all the regions and provinces."

ARTICLE-109

"1ˢᵗ – The federal government will administer oil and gas extracted from current fields in cooperation with the governments of the producing regions and provinces on condition that the revenues will be distributed fairly in a manner compatible with the demographical distribution all over the country. A quota should be defined for a specified time for affected regions that were deprived in an unfair way by the former regime or later on, in a way to ensure balanced development in different parts of the country.
"This should be regulated by law."

Article-108 stated only oil and gas without referring to the other natural resources such as mercury in Al Emara (Misan) province and sulfur in Kirkuk and Geyyara and other valuable minerals in northern Iraq. Article-109 stated that, "a quota should be defined for a specified time for affected regions that were deprived in an unfair way by the former regime or later on, in a way to ensure balanced development in different parts of the country."

As a matter of fact all Iraqi provinces were affected by the former Iraqi regime. The oil and gas revenue distribution is not specified in the draft. It is also affirmed that law should regulate this distribution. However, since the law was not specified in the draft, it means that the future of Kirkuk, Mosul, Khanakin and Basra will remain uncertain.

ARTICLE-111

"All that is not written in the exclusive powers of the federal authorities is in the authority of the regions. In other powers shared between the federal government and the regions, the priority will be given to the region's law in case of dispute."

This indicates that the regional government will have more power and authority. This will facilitate the division of Iraq in the near future.

ARTICLE-121

"This constitution guarantees the administrative, political, cultural, educational rights for the various ethnicities such as Turkmen, Chaldeans, Assyrians, and the other components, and this is regulated through a law."

This is another indication that the Turkmen were treated as a minority and listed among the others. They were not considered as the third largest ethnic group beside Arabs and Kurds. However, the law to guarantee the Turkmen rights is not specified yet.

ARTICLE-136

"1st – The executive authority will take the necessary steps to complete implementation of the requirements of Article (58) of the Transitional Administration Law for the Iraqi State, with all its clauses.

"2nd – The responsibilities placed on the executive authority provided for in Article (58) of the Transitional Administration Law for the Iraqi State are extended to and will continue for the executive authority until the completion of (normalization, census, ending with a census in Kirkuk and other disputed areas to determine the will of the people) in a period no longer than 12/31/2007."

Indeed, the Turkmen are not entirely opposing Article 58 of the previous Transitional Administration Law, but this law should be applied under certain circumstances. The Turkmen strongly believe that this article will provide enough time for the Kurdish parties to settle thousands of non-Kirkuk residents in the city. This will eventually increase the Kurdish population and then will unjustly determine the future of Kirkuk with the proposed referendum at the end of 2007.

One can clearly see that the Turkmen were totally excluded from the committee of normalization in Kirkuk. Furthermore, the leader of the Iraqi Communist Party, Hamit Musa, was appointed as the head of the committee. Musa is known for having close ties with the Kurdish parties. As mentioned earlier, the Iraqi Communist Party and KDP were behind the massacre of Turkmen in July 14,1959 where many Turkmen were killed. Despite the fact that Kirkuk is a Turkmen city, Turkmen parties were always underestimated in determining the future of Kirkuk.

The Turkmen proposal in this matter is to implement the article according to the 1957 census or according to the food stamps that

General Sabah Kara Altun, a Turkmen, was assasinated in Kirkuk in 2005.

were distributed according to this census in Kirkuk. These two conditions will absolutely prove the Turkmen identity of Kirkuk and will determine the original population distribution in the city. The Kurds that were brought into Kirkuk after April 9, 2003 should depart the city to their previous places.

ARTICLE-138

> *"The Transitional Administration Law for the Iraqi State and its appendix are voided upon creation of the new government, except for what appears in paragraph (a) of Article (53) and Article (58) of the Transitional Administration Law."*

Paragraph (c) of Article-53 of the Transitional Administration Law gives Kirkuk and Baghdad a special status and opposes their annexation to any region. Cancelling this paragraph in the draft constitution is a clear indication that Kirkuk will be annexed to the northern Kurdish region, which the Turkmen and Arabs strongly opposed.

The draft constitution should give Kirkuk a special status because it is considered as a multi-ethnic city representing all Iraqi segments. Despite the fact that the administrative, cultural and political rights of the Turkmen were said to be guaranteed, it is not possible to say that the law is satisfactory at these points. The Turkmen, by this constitution, feel that they will be assimilated sooner in Iraq. We strongly believe that after 2007 it will not be possible even to name the region of Turkmeneli nor the Turkmen nation.

After carefully reviewing the draft constitution, the Iraqi Turkmen Front's position was a "NO" vote in the referendum that was held on October 15, 2005.

ANTICIPATED IRREGULARITIES IN SECOND ELECTION

The irregularities that occurred in Kirkuk during the referendum of October 15, 2005 over the draft constitution are expected to reoccur in the next election. On August 7, 2005 the Turkmen parties delivered their written concern to the IECI about the new procedure in Kirkuk that allowed the non-residents of Kirkuk to register in the city.Once again the Kurdish parties brought thousands of non-residents from Sulaimaniyah, Erbil and Dohuk to register in Kirkuk and also for the future referendum to determine the identity of the city at the end of 2007.

It is very obvious that there has been a tremendous increase in the voters' number in Kirkuk compared to the previous Iraqi elections. It has been observed that this number is about one-fourth of the entire Iraqi voter turnout. Compared to Baghdad, there were 10 times as many voters in Kirkuk.We are wondering how the number of the voters in Kirkuk has increased while the population of the city remained unchanged (the population of Kirkuk in April 2003 was 830,000). There were 227,000 additional voters in Kirkuk after the elections of January 30, 2005.

On top of that, the IECI was aware of the situation that made Dr. Farid Ayyar delete 86,000 voters from the list (Kurds who came from northern Kurdish provinces to register and vote more than once in Kirkuk). He also indicated that the number of the voters during the elections of January 2005 was 576,048 while it was increased to 691,581 during the referendum of October 15, 2005. As well, for the election, the IECI appointed 12 Kurds, seven Arabs and only five Turkmen as directors of polling centres in Kirkuk – once again violating the Turkmen majority rights in the city.

Recently the Kurdish governor of Kirkuk, Abdurrahman Mustafa, authorized all entry point officials to allow Kurdish families to enter and settle in the city. As such, thousands of Kurdish families, who were given fake displacement letters, had entered Kirkuk and an abnormal increase in the Kurdish population was noticed.

IRAQ'S SECOND ELECTION, DECEMBER 2005

Manipulations and irregularities committed by the Kurds in Kirkuk during the elections of December 15, 2005:

1. Following the decision made by the IECI to allow 227,000 Kurds to vote, Kirkuk was thrown into chaos with this population creating unrest and disturbances across the city. Flag-waving Kurdish convoys

went out into the Turkmen and Arab districts hurling slogans and intimidating the locals.

2. Kurdish poll workers and observers allowed thousands of underage Kurds vote more than once in Kirkuk and other Turkmen regions. Images of this were recorded by Turkmeneli TV.

3. Designated voter-registration and polling stations were kept open for the Kurdish security forces. Approximately 10,000 peshmergas were brought from Chamchamal (located north of Kirkuk on Sulaimaniyah major road) and Erbil to secure the voting stations. Although segments of both the Kurdish ING members and peshmergas were found to have voted more than once in some occasions, they called the coalition forces in Kirkuk when the Turkmen police members tried to vote. The forces disarmed the Turkmen police and stopped them from voting.

4. Many Turkmen male and female workers were intimidated and beaten by the Kurdish Iraqi Police and ING, particularly in El Shorija, Iskan and Raheem Awa districts. In addition, these two security forces encouraged the local inhabitants to attack the Turkmen in the region.

5. The Kurdish IP and ING had encouraged and forced the people in Kirkuk to vote for the Kurdish coalition list 730. They also threatened to arrest anyone that refused.

6. The Kurds intentionally did not provide the following Turkmen

Kurdish governor Abdurrahman Mustafa ordered all entry point officials to allow Kurdish families to enter Kirkuk if they were holding fake displacement letters such as this one.

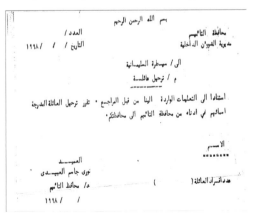

regions with the list of the Turkmen voters who had voted in the last elections. This action resulted in losing thousands of Turkmen votes in Hay Al Wasiti, 1- Haziran, Al Kadisiyah, Arafa, Korya, Tisin, Dibis, Musalla and Tuz Hurmatu.

7.   While the ballot papers for the Kurdish regions were fully prepared, the ballot papers for the Turkmen districts were all incomplete.

8. Despite the regulations to prevent security forces including the IP, ING and Petrol Protecting Police Force to vote during the elections, thousands of Kurdish IP, ING and security forces voted more than once. It was decided by the IECI that the security forces should vote one day earlier in the elections.

9. The Kurdish IP and ING were carrying Kurdish flags in Kirkuk to provoke and intimidate the non-Kurdish segments in the city.

10. The Kurdish IP and ING forcibly prevented Turkmen observers from monitoring fraudulent activities in the election centres in Kirkuk as the Kurds were voting more than once. This was observed specifically in the Tisin Turkmen district in the city.

11.   The transportation badges were unfairly distributed between the different segments in Kirkuk with the Kurds holding the majority.

12.   Thousands of Turkmen voters' names were intentionally deleted from the ballot papers in many Turkmen districts.

13.   Despite the fact the IECI found forgeries in Kirkuk, the Commission issued an order for 227,000 Kurds to vote in the elections. The IECI has announced that a printing mistake was made during the preparations of the voters list. This was also affirmed by Ferhad Talabani, a Kurdish PUK member and Kirkuk IECI director. As well, the Kurds threatened to use other tactics to restore the 86,000 Kurds that were cancelled by the IECI.

14.   Another example of Kurdish IP and ING atrocities was when Turkmen observer Gazi Hussain was harshly abused by Kurdish Colonel Azad from Raheem Awa police station in front of Howraman polling station. It was also reported that Colonel Azad had encouraged his police companions to abuse other Turkmen observers as well.

15. Thousands of Kurds used different tactics to vote more than once. Some covered their index finger with ointments and others used different paint removers such as liquid detergent.

16. The Kurdish officials stopped people from entering Asma Bint Abubakir election centre in Kirkuk.

17. The Kurdish IECI officials and poll workers provided Kurdish voters with more than one ballot paper.

18. Kurdish militia forces entered the election centres in Kirkuk and threatened the observers from different political bodies not to report the forgeries. For example, this action took place in Diyar Bakir centre in Al Shuhada-Hurriya district.

19. In a front page story written by Somajeh Gheminia in the Dutch newspaper *Trouw* on December 15, 2005, the article posted the forgeries in the Iraqi Election Out of Country Voting Program (OCV) with four pictures indicating how easy it was to remove the ink used in the elections. According to the article, it could be removed within seconds by using household bleach. S.G Tahir from IECI-OCV later denied these allegations and insisted that the election ink was difficult to remove. He also said that he would investigate the situation.

20. Other negative acts committed by the Kurdish police and ING included the arrest of a group of male and female Iraqi Turkmen Front observers who were detained in a police station under the charge that they were carrying fake badges. Despite their attempts to prove that the badges were official, they were detained until the end of the election. It can only be assumed that this action was done to prevent observers from the ITF to trace and report the fraudulent activities committed by the Kurds in Kirkuk.

21. Many Turkmen observers were abused, beaten and insulted by the Kurdish IP and ING. These forces encouraged the local Kurds to do this as well. In one example, Kurdish police officer Akram Omar had arrested several Turkmen observers in Girnata election centre in Kirkuk and detained them for more than four hours.

22. In Ata Begler voting centre, in 1-Huzairan district, a Kurdish police officer from Miqdad police station arrested Mrs. Ganiye Garip, a prominent Turkmen and ITF observer. She was arrested for

several hours under the suspicion of false identification. Therefore the Kurdish poll workers, observers and station managers all took advantage of the Turkmen observers' absence and allowed the Kurdish voters to vote more than once in each polling station in Kirkuk and other Turkmen areas.

23. Kurdish voters in Shorija district attacked the vehicles carrying the Turkmen voters and observers. The vehicle windows were smashed and many were severely injured. At the same station, the Kurds attacked observers from the ITF after they reported illegal actions. Before letting them leave the election centres, the Kurds seized the observers' belongings, which included documents concerning these actions.

24. The Kurdish police forces strongly supported Kurdish voters. They were also assisting the Kurdish party representatives in distributing bribes ($50 USD) for the Kurdish coalition list 730 voters.

25. Prior to the elections, the Kurds launched an attack on the Turkmen satellite TV (Turkmeneli TV). Their intention was to stop broadcasting the election promotional activities for the Iraqi Turkmen Front.

26. Ferhad Talabani was appointed as the director of the IECI in Kirkuk. He put all his efforts for the favour of the Kurdish coalition list 730.

27. Forty Turkmen observers from the ITF were beaten and not allowed to enter the polling stations in Shorija, Raheem Awa, Almas and Iskan.

28. Prior to the election, the Kurdish IP and ING raided the Kara Altun and Kale Iraqi Turkmen Front bureau and offices and the guarding weapons were confiscated.

29. Extra polling stations were opened for the Kurds at the police emergency forces building in Hay Al Baas.

30. Following the election, Sabah Salahaddin, a Turkmen observer from the ITF, was kidnapped and two days later his body was found in Raheem Awa district.

31. Prior to the election, Turkmen teenager Mohammed Sabah was killed on duty after the ITF office in Almas was raided.

32. The Asaish confiscated two trucks carrying election materials for the ITF that were printed in Turkey. The two trucks passed the border at Ibrahim Halil border gate after presenting the proper documents.

33. The Kurds and Kurdish IP attacked Turkmen female poll workers in Shorija and Imam Kasim Kurdish-dominated districts. An eyewitness reported that the IP encouraged the Kurds to attack vehicles carrying Turkmen observers and poll workers. Many Turkmen females were injured during the attack.

34. Many Kurdish IECI officials in Kirkuk allowed people whose names were not in the primary or additional lists to vote.

35. In order to prevent the Turkmen observers from reporting the illegal acts, many Kurdish election centre managers prevented them from obtaining official complaint forms.

36. Many ballot boxes were stolen and replaced by new ballot papers in favour of Kurdish coalition list 730. An official complaint letter was sent to İzzeddin El Muhammad, an official in the IECI, regarding the irregularities committed in Kirkuk. İzzeddin El Muhammad declared that the IECI would soon take all official complaints into consideration. He also declared that the stolen ballot boxes would be the responsibility of the Interior Ministry. This could potentially indicate the lack of security in Kirkuk in particular and in Iraq in general. It would also inform officials where the ballot boxes were taken and who counted the ballots.

37. According to Kirkuk city council member Hassan Turan, the Turkmen will forward all irregularities committed by the Kurds to the IECI and they will demand a new election. He also demanded the active involvement of the United Nations in Kirkuk and other Turkmen regions. Hassan Turan said the non-Kurds in Kirkuk were unable to locate their names in the ballot lists because the names of the Turkmen were deliberately deleted.

38. Kirkuk governor Abdurrahman Mustafa had complained about the number of the election posters printed in Turkish and Arabic. He declared that the number of posters in Turkish and Arabic exceeded those written in Kurdish.

The Turkmen Council in Kirkuk, which consists of 74 members, wondered why the governor was only complaining about this topic and not the other fraudulent and unjust acts against the Turkmen by the Kurds in the city.

39. In Tuz Hurmatu (roughly 44 kilometres south of Kirkuk) the polling stations were closed to the Turkmen at 11:00 a.m., while the Kurds were allowed to vote more than once.

40. In Altun Kopru the Kurds replaced Turkmen observers and voters identifying members. The Kurdish police and ING were escorting hundreds of buses carrying Kurdish voters from Erbil.

41. The Kurdish police had arrested only Turkish Cihan News Agency correspondents in Kirkuk in front of the other foreign correspondents.

42. Adil Allami, an IECI executive board member, had conducted a meeting in Kirkuk with the political party leaders regarding the procedures of the election. The following parties and communities had asked for a new election in Kirkuk due to the numerous irregularities committed by the Kurds:

    A) Iraqi Turkmen Front
    B) Party of Turkmenel
    C) Badir Organization
    D) Arab Community
    E) Arab Tribes Committee

EVENTS THAT OCCURRED AFTER THE ELECTION

On December 18, 2005 the IECI issued an order to cancel the election in Karatepe-Khanakin in Diyalah province due to the irregularities committed. This order was published on the Iraq News Agency website on the same day.

On December 27, 2005, more than 75 Turkmen and Arab politicians and noblemen conducted a meeting in Kirkuk over the initial results of the elections. They demanded an international investigation into the results. The chairman of the Arab council, Abdurrahman Munshed Al-Asi, declared that the reason of this meeting was to convoy the message of the Turkmen and the Arabs to the United States and the

United Nations over the unfair elections in Kirkuk. He also declared that the results were influenced by the dominate political parties, such as the Kurds especially in Kirkuk. Abdurrahman Al-Asi also accused the IECI of assisting the Kurds and said that the IECI allowed the registration of more than 227,000 Kurds who were not from Kirkuk.

MARAM ESTABLISHED

MARAM (an Arabic word translated to mean political parties objecting the results of the election) is a coalition of political parties who strongly rejected the election results of December 15, 2005. The collective is led by the top Sunni Arabs and has increased from 26 to 143 different Iraqi parties. Together, the organization has threatened to boycott Iraq's next parliament and warned of a surge in violence if new nationwide elections are not held. As well, a secular coalition led by former interim Prime Minister Iyad Allawi issued a statement denouncing the latest election as fraudulent and listed demands they said must be met before they would participate in the new legislature.

Yasar Abdullah from the ITF declared large groups who had militia forces dominated the voting centres by force, which worked to their benefit. He also declared that the IECI should prevent the uncivilized methods used during the elections. Therefore we are here to prove our loyalty to Iraq first and then to sustain our support to the patriotic Iraqi forces who are seeking the unity and integrity of Iraq. We will continue to expose the irregularities committed during the elections by using the democratic ways and we will do our best for new elections in the places where Turkmen, Arabs and Kurds live.

MARAM organized a news conference in Baghdad attended by representatives from most of the parties involved and stated that "we will not have any other choice but to boycott the political process and the coming parliament. This would lead to more struggle and bloody violence and threat to the Iraqi entity and its people." More than 1,500 complaints have been made, including 39 deemed serious enough to affect results, according to election officials.

"How could we build an Iraq with a fraudulent process?"

demanded Ayham Samarraie, who heads the Independent Iraqis Gathering, a Sunni party. The call for new elections emerged from two days of talks at Allawi's Baghdad office. The Tawafaq Front, a coalition led by the Iraqi Islamic Party, widely considered the largest Sunni Arab party, and the Iraqi Front for National Dialogue, led by Sunni hardliner Saleh Mutlak, were among the groups involved in the talks. The parties that signed the statement appear to have won as many as 80 seats in the 275-seat National Assembly, according to an analysis of preliminary results. "We were all surprised by the forgery and fraud in the election process," the statement said. "If these violations pass without a punishment, they will empower a phoney democracy that's closer to a dictatorship."

IRAQIS PROTEST ELECTION RESULTS
Thousands of Iraqis in different cities – Baghdad, Tikrit, Rumadi, Mosul, Diyalah and Kirkuk – have demonstrated against the results of the elections and called for the independent role of the IECI, rather than being instructed by the powerful political parties who have militia groups such as the peshmergas (Kurdish militias in the north) and the Badir forces (Shiite militia in the south). They also demanded the involvement of the international community to investigate the results and the repetition of the election in Iraq.

In Kirkuk thousands of Turkmen, Arabs and Assyrians have protested the results of the elections. The protestors were carrying pan cards with written slogans calling for new elections and also the unity of Iraq and to stop differentiating between the Sunni and Shiites sects in Iraq.

THE DESIRES OF THE TURKMEN IN IRAQ

1. A humanitarian democratic system must be established.

2. The disarmament of the Kurdish forces particularly in Kirkuk and all over Iraq.

3. Police and security forces should be equally represented by all ethnicities in Iraq and particularly in Kirkuk (Turkmen, Arabs, Kurds and Assyrians). Kurds are dominating police divisions and security

forces in Kirkuk. The armed forces and the police must be independent and they should take orders from the central government in Baghdad, not from political parties and groups.

4. All discrimination and injustices based on ethnic background and religious convictions must stop.

5. The Iraqi Turkmen Front, representing 90 per cent of the Turkmen in Iraq, should have an active role in the future government of Iraq and also in Kirkuk city council.

6. All Kurdish families who do not belong to Kirkuk should leave the city, particularly those that came after April 10, 2003.

7. Turkmen employees who were expelled by the Kurds should return to their jobs.

8. All Turkmen detainees must be released immediately. Over 400 Arabs and Turkmen were detained by the Kurdish forces and were detained in Erbil and Sulaimaniyah prisons.

9. Kurdish flags should be replaced with Iraqi flags.

10. The unlimited Kurdish parties' bases should been limited in Kirkuk.

11. In order to prove the actual Turkmen population, a general census monitored by the coalition forces and United Nations should be performed.

12. All Turkmen villages should be rebuilt and the original owners should be returned and compensated.

13. The Turkmen people of Iraq as well as the other Iraqi segments should be given the right to preserve their ethnic heritage and cultural identity.

14. All former Ba'ath regime buildings that caused pain and suffering to Iraqis should be demolished and replaced with entertainment parks.

15. The Turkmen should be mentioned in the constitution as the third major segment of Iraq beside the Arabs and the Kurds.

16. Turkmen language should be stated as an official language beside Arabic and Kurdish.

17. Turkmen should have an active role in the future government of Iraq.

18. If the proposed federal system is implemented, and recognized by all Iraqis, then the Turkmen should be given the right to have their own federal region called Turkmeneli.

19. In Transitional Administration Law and the new Iraqi constitution, the Turkmen rights were denied and subjected to negligence. The Turkmen are calling for:

A) The guarantee of the use of the Turkmen language as an official language in Iraq besides Arabic and Kurdish.

B) The guarantee of teaching the Turkmen language in public and private schools in areas where the Turkmen population is densely settled.

C) The guarantee of all Turkmen political, administrative, educational, economical and cultural rights.

D) The Turkmen identity of Kirkuk city should be preserved and should be given a special status with Baghdad as indicated in subject 53-C in the interim constitution and to prevent any attempts to annex it to the Kurdish region. The proposed referendum regarding the future of Kirkuk in the end of 2007 should be nationally performed. It is stated in the Article 136 that the future of Kirkuk should be determined by the referendum only in Kirkuk. Article 136 -2 reads: "The responsibilities placed on the executive authority provided for in Article (58) of the Transitional Administration Law for the Iraqi State are extended to and will continue for the executive authority until the completion of (normalization, census, ending with a census in Kirkuk and other disputed areas to determine the will of the people) in a period no longer than 12/31/2007." However, the issue of Kirkuk should be determined by all Iraqis, not only the residents of Kirkuk. The demographical shape of Kirkuk was altered twice; first due to the Arabification policy and secondly by the Kurds after April 10, 2003.

CONCLUSION: IMPROVED RELATIONS

Turkmen-Kurdish relations could be improved under the following circumstances:

1. The Kurds should recognize the Turkmen region that is called Turkmeneli – starting from Telafer in the northwest to Mendeli in the southeast of Iraq including Kirkuk as a capital. This request is not to separate the Turkmen region – the Turkmen always requested land and national unity of Iraq.

2. They should completely pull out of the Turkmen regions and cities such as Kirkuk, Hanakin, Mendeli, Bedre, Kifri, Karatepe and Erbil which were considered as Turkmen cities until the Kurdish invasion in the late-1980s.

3. They should equally recognize the legitimate rights of the Turkmen living in some Kurdish areas, such as the Turkmen involvement in the regional parliament and government as well as the regional revenue.

4. Full and immediate release of all Turkmen detainees and prisoners.

5. The Kurds should work with all Iraqi segments and particularly with the Turkmen for land and national unity of Iraq.

6. The Kurds should stop the desire to establish an independent Kurdish state. This will divide Iraq and the region and would open the door for other Iraqi segments to request the same desire. This would also encourage the neighboring countries to intervene.

7. The Kurds should stop taking a hostile and combative attitude towards the Turkmen.

8. The Kurds should treat the Turkmen in the north as partners rather than minorities. They have been putting in a lot of effort to treat the Turkmen as a minority.

9. There should be fair administration in the Kurdish provinces where the Turkmen exist.

10. Officially, the Kurds occupy high positions in the Iraqi interim government and as such should act independently and work for Iraq in general. On top of that they should also stop initiating provocative acts and declarations.

11. The Turkmen should administer densely Turkmen populated cities, such as Kirkuk, with respect to other minorities. The governor

and the mayor of Kirkuk should be a Turkmen.

12. The Kurdish parties PUK and KDP should stop supporting the puppet parties acting on behalf of the Turkmen. (Puppet parties are groups established by the two Kurdish parties to approve the policies of KDP and PUK. The puppet parties are in the state of rivalry with the Iraqi Turkmen Front. KDP has established eight, while the PUK supports three puppet parties).

13. The Kurdish parties should stop supporting the PKK, which is listed among the terrorist groups issued by U.S.A. Ten-thousand PKK members with their families were brought into Kirkuk and provided fake Iraqi national identity cards and had participated in the general elections of January 31, 2005 and December 15, 2005. The PKK in Iraq has formed a new party called the Kurdistan Freedom and Democracy Congress (KADEK) and actively performed their political activities in Kirkuk.

14. Kirkuk should be given a special status and should not be annexed to any region. All of Iraq's 18 provinces should determine the future of Kirkuk in the referendum of 2007, not only the people of Kirkuk.

15. The city of Kirkuk should be normalized according to the census of 1957.

The Turkmen had never been against the Kurds throughout history. They always extended support to the Kurds, but the Kurds are forcing the Turkmen to accept their policies, recognize the word "Kurdistan," and take over the Turkmen region, most specifically, Kirkuk. Moreover, the Kurds are rejecting the political presence of the Turkmen in northern Iraq particularly the Iraqi Turkmen Front and all the Turkmen parties gathered under its umbrella.

The Turkmen believe, however, there is no such land as Kurdistan, it is called northern Iraq. If there were a Kurdistan there should also be Turkmen Land, Arabistan and Assyrian Land – such partitioning would ultimately end up dividing Iraq into small states. Iraq was always a unified country and all Iraqi segments lived together in peace and harmony throughout history.

APPENDIX

AN ABRIDGED HISTORY OF IRAQ

ANCIENT MESOPOTAMIA

SUMER (3500BC – 2400BC)

The ancient empire of Sumer was located in the region of southern Mesopotamia. Although there are no exact dates recorded, it is believed that the first Turkmen presence settled in Mesopotamia around 3500BC. Sumer was a linguistic and ethnic mosaic that included earlier inhabitants of the region. Initially, the Turkmen involved in this first phase of migration resisted assimilation. However, over the passage of time, the relatively small Turkic tribes became absorbed by the more numerous indigenous population. Considered to be the "Cradle of Civilization," the Sumerians were the first people known to have devised a scheme of written representation as a means of communication. The most important political development of this era was the emergence of kings, who exercised absolute political authority over the Sumerian city-states.

AKKAD (2400BC – 2200BC)

Sumer was conquered in 2334BC by Sargon I, king of the Semitic city of Akkad. To ensure his supremacy, Sargon created the first conscripted army, a development necessitated by the need to mobilize large numbers of labourers for irrigation and flood-control works. The fall of the Akkadians was caused by the re-emergence of the Sumerians, under the King of Ur, who briefly established hegemony over much of Mesopotamia. However, by 2000BC, combined attacks by the Amorites, a Semitic people from the west, and the Elamites, a Caucasian

people from the east, had destroyed the Third Dynasty of Ur. The invaders, nevertheless, retained much of the Sumerian-Akkadian political and cultural legacy.

BABYLON (2000BC – 539BC)

The Amorites, a prosperous nomadic tribe, emerged as the dominant political power sometime before 2000BC and established cities on the Tigris and the Euphrates rivers. They chose Babylon, a town to the north, as their capital. However, widespread migration of tribes from central Asia would soon destabilize the Babylonian empire. Around 1600BC, Indo-European-speaking tribes invaded India; while other tribes settled in Iran and eastern Europe. One of these groups, the Hittites, allied itself with the Kassites, a warlike, nomadic people of unknown origins. Together, they conquered and destroyed Babylon. After 800BC, the Semitic-speaking Assyrians from northern Mesopotamia embarked on a policy of expansion. In 612BC, revolts of subject peoples combined with the allied forces of two new kingdoms, those of the Medes and the Chaldeans (Neo-Babylonians), to effectively end Assyrian rule. This new regime would last just half a century before falling to yet another invader, the Persian King Cyrus the Great who captured Babylon and added Mesopotamia to his empire in the year 539 B.C.

PERSIAN AND GREEK INTRUSIONS

(551BC – 331BC)

Persian Iranian rule lasted for more than 200 years, from 551BC – 331BC. During this time, large numbers of Persian tribes were added to Mesopotamia's ethnically diverse population. Persian rule ended at the hands of Alexander the Great who led a Greek army into Iraq. After his death in 311BC his empire was divided. Iraq was the share of Seleicus who established the Seleviad dynasty with his capital at Babylon. In the centuries to come, the Pathian, Persians, and Sasanians would occupy the Cradle of Civilization. Eventually the city of Babylon would lose its preeminence as the center of the civilized world as political and economic activity shifted to the Mediterranean and Rome.

ARAB CONQUEST AND THE COMING OF ISLAM

Islamic forays into Iraq began during the reign of Caliph Abu Bakr. In 634AD, an army of 18,000 Arab tribesmen, reached the delta of the Tigris and Euphrates. Although the occupying Persian force was vastly superior in tactics and numbers, its soldiers were exhausted from their unremitting campaigns against the Byzantines. Many of the Iraqi tribes were Christian at the time of the Islamic conquest. By 650AD, Muslim armies under the command of Ubaydullah Bin Ziyad had reached the Amu Darya (Oxus River) and had conquered all of Mesopotamia. One of the keys to Bin Ziyad's success was the use of Turkmen archers from Central Asia. Following the conquest of Mesopotamia, approximately 2000 Turkmen soldiers were deployed around Basra.

THE ABBASID CALIPHATE (750–1055)

During the reign of the first seven Caliphs, Baghdad became the centre of power where Arab and Persian cul-

tures merged. This era is remembered throughout the Arab world and by Iraqis in particular, as the pinnacle of the Islamic past. Turkish recruitment into the army strengthened the Abbasid Caliphate. Caliph Al Mansour (754-775) established a regiment consisting entirely of Turkmen. These troops continued to have a growing influence in the Abbasid army. More than 70,000 Turkmen troops with their families settled in Baghdad under the Caliphs.

THE SELJUK-PERIOD (1055–1258)

The Seljuks are originally from the Oguz Turkic tribes of Central Asia. These Turkmen had established a great empire from India to Egypt and from the west coast of Turkey to Oman. The Seljuk Empire was extended to Syria and Palestine in 1089, During this period many Turkmen dynasties were established and Turkmen families were settled in the Tavuk region, south of Kirkuk. Ruling from their capital in Baghdad, the Seljuk's controlled the lands from the Bosphorus to Chinese Turkestan until approximately 1155. The Seljuks continued to expand their territories, but they were content to let the local tribesmen simply pay tribute while administering and ruling their own lands. Tughril (1177-94), the last Seljuk sultan of Iraq, was killed by the leader of another Turkic dynasty, the Khwarizm Shah. Before his could establish his rule, however, Iraq was overrun by the Mongol horde.

THE MONGOL INVASION

In the early years of the thirteenth century, a powerful Mongol leader named Temujin brought together an alliance of the Mongol tribes and led them on a devastating sweep through China, eastern Europe and the Middle East. In

Mesopotamia, political chaos, severe economic depression, and social disintegration followed in the wake of the Mongol invasions. Baghdad, once the centre of a great empire, rapidly lost its importance. Basra, which had been a key transit point for global sea trade, was circumvented after the Portuguese found an alternative maritime route to Asia around Cape of Good Hope. By the end of the Mongol period, the focus of Mesopotamian society had shifted from the urban foundation of the Abbasid culture to the tribes of the river valleys.

THE OTTOMAN PERIOD (1534–1914)

In the years following the Mongol invasion, Turkmen tribes from Iran, the Safavids, struggled for control of Iraq with the advancing Ottomans under Suleiman the Magnificent. Baghdad fell to Suleiman in 1534. The Ottomans divided Iraq into four provinces which they would govern until the First World War. One major impact of the Safavid-Ottoman conflict on Iraqi history was the deepening of the Shia-Sunni religious divisions. Another important development during this period was the aggressive expansion of European colonial and economic interests in the Middle East. The British had established a consulate at Baghdad in 1802, and a French consulate followed shortly thereafter. European interest in modernizing Iraq to facilitate Western commercial interests coincided with Ottoman reforms. In 1908, a new ruling clique, the Young Turks, took power in Istanbul. They stressed secular politics and patriotism over the pan-Islamic ideology preached by Sultan Abd al Hamid. However, the Turkish Empire was in a slow decline. By the early 20th century, the once powerful Ottoman Empire was referred to as the "Sick Old Man of Europe."

MODERN IRAQ

1914 – In order to protect its oil interests in neighbouring Iran, the British launch an offensive into Mesopotamia against the Ottoman Turks.

1915 – After some success against the Turks near Basra, the British expeditionary forces push north where they suffer a devastating defeat at the city of Kut.

1917 – With additional reinforcements and the assistance of Arab allies, the Turks are pushed out of Mesopotamia and the British occupy the provinces of Basra and Baghdad.

1918 – Although it was not previously known that the Turk-occupied Mesopotamian provinces possessed oil resources, by the end of World War I British naval engineers had determined that this region contained "the world's largest deposits." At the end of hostilities, the Turkish army still controlled the province of Mosul, including Kirkuk. However, in the post war collapse of the Ottoman Empire. The British violated the armistice and occupied the rest of Mesopotamia.

1919 – With proven oil reserves located in Basra, the British hesitate on turning this region over to the Arabs as they had previously promised.

1920 – After being snubbed by both Britain and France, Faisal I declares himself the King of Syria and his brother Abdullah is named the King of Mesopotamia. The French and British suppress Faisal and ignore Abdullah, setting in motion a regional wave of violence and anarchy.

1921 – Unable to suppress the revolt in Mesopotamia, the exiled King Faisal I is recalled from Lebanon and proclaimed 'King' of the newly created State of Iraq.

1924 – Nestorian levies besiege Kirkuk

and massacre Turkmen citizens.

1927 – The natural gas fires of Baba Gurgur are finally explored and the oil deposits of northern Iraq are proven to be among the world's richest.

1932 – King Faisal I attains Iraq's independence from Britain. Iraq is admitted into the League of Nations, but British troops and aircraft remain in the country which has now been declared a protectorate.

1938 – Oil is discovered in the sheikdom of Kuwait and Faisal's son, King Ghazi, lays claim to this territory as Iraq's 19th province. With both Kuwait and Iraq under British protection, the issue of Kuwait's appropriation is soon dropped.

1939 – King Ghazi is killed in a suspicious automobile accident. His three-year-old son, Faisal II, assumes the throne with his uncle, Abdul Illah, serving as regent.

1941 – At the height of World War II, with British troops stretched thin around the globe, Iraqi military officers stage a rebellion. The British rush reinforcements from India and Palestine to restore Faisal II's monarchy and secure British oil investments.

1958 – General Abdul Karim Kassem stages a military coup on July 14th. King Faisal II is killed and the last of the British troops are withdrawn from Iraq.

1959 – On July 14th, the first anniversary of President Kassem's coup, the Kurds stage an ambush against Turkmen celebrating in Kirkuk. Over a three-day period, hundreds of Turkmen were wounded and several dozens killed.

1963 – With the backing of the CIA, the Ba'ath Party seizes power briefly. In the wake of the coup, President Kassem and thousands of his followers are slaughtered.

1968 – Although they had in turn been ousted from power by a military junta, the Ba'athists regain control of Iraq. As deputy to President Ahmet Hassan Alba-kir, a young Saddam Hussein was seen as the controlling force in Iraq.

1972 – Iraq nationalizes its oil resources and calls on other Arab nations to do the same.

1973 – The Organization of Petroleum Exporting Countries (OPEC) raises prices to protest America's support of Israel in the Yom Kippur War. This sets the U.S. economy into turmoil.

1975 – After the CIA and the Shah of Iran had successfully supported a Kurdish rebellion in Iraq, Saddam signed a treaty in Algeria. In exchange for Iran's use of the Shatt al-Arab waterway, Iraq's military was allowed a free hand to crush the Kurds.

1979 – Saddam Hussein becomes President of Iraq at the same time the Shah of Iran is toppled. With Shiite fundamentalists in control of Iran, Saddam is encouraged by the U.S. to declare war against the Ayatollah Khomeini.

1980 – Saddam believes his forces can easily defeat the Iranian army since it had been recently purged of its officer corps. However, after only limited initial gains, the Iraqi offensive bogs down into a war of attrition.

1984 – With his forces pushed back against the Shatt al-Arab, Saddam indicates he will end the war. President Ronald Reagan's special envoy, Donald Rumsfeld, flies to Baghdad. Saddam is promised full U.S. support – including chemical weaponry.

1988 – Iran and Iraq sign a peace agreement. The Pentagon begins conducting war games based on the scenario that Iraq has attacked Kuwait.

1990 – Forced to repay Kuwait a $30 billion loan yet unable to increase oil prices,

Iraq issues an ultimatum to Kuwait to cease its overproduction of oil. The U.S. advises Saddam that it has no position on Arab-Arab affairs. On August 2, Iraq invades Kuwait. Four days later the UN Security Council imposes sanctions against Iraq. On August 7, George Bush Sr. launches Operation *Desert Shield*.

1991 – On January 17, the U.S.-led coalition initiates 48 days of airstrikes against Iraq and occupied Kuwait. On February 24, the ground assault goes in and Saddam's forces are routed. Four days later, Iraq signs a ceasefire agreement with the coalition forces. With the collapse of his army, Saddam faces rebellion within Iraq. After months of heavy fighting, Saddam regains 15 of his 18 provinces; the three northern provinces remain under the control of Kurdish rebels. Many innocent Turkmen were forced to flee their homes and 135 were killed in Altun Kopru by Iraqi forces.

1996 – Saddam assists Kurdish warlord Massoud Barzani in an incursion into the territory controlled by rival Kurd, Jalal Talabani. KDP and Iraqi forces attacked ITF offices and killed almost 130 people.

2001 – On February 17, newly elected President George W. Bush sends a message to Saddam in the form of airstrikes. The world condemns the U.S. aggression. On September 11, the U.S. suffers a devastating terror attack. Saddam issues a statement proclaiming that America has "reaped what it has sown." Although Osama bin Laden is the primary suspect, Bush warns Saddam to "watch his step."

2002 – On August 15, the U.S. Joint Chiefs of Staff approve a strategic plan to invade Iraq. On October 15, Saddam stages a presidential referendum and wins a 100 per cent majority.

2003 – On March 20, coalition forces begin their attack on Iraq. On April 9, with the pulling of Saddam Hussein's statue, the Ba'athist regime comes to an end. After the Iraqi army resistance collapses, Kurdish troops enter Mosul and Kirkuk. The peshmerga are intent on burning all government records such as birth certificates and land registry titles. In the absence of law and order, widespread looting and arson erupts throughout Iraq. On May 2, interim U.S. military governor Jay Garner is replaced by former diplomat Paul Bremer. On December 13, Saddam Hussein is captured near Tikrit by U.S. special forces.

2004 – On June 3, newly appointed Prime Minister Iyad Allawi announces his new cabinet. Only one Turkmen is named to the 30-member council and is not a representative from the ITF. On June 28, the U.S. authorities hand over power to Allawi's interim Iraqi council.

2005 – On January 30, Ibrahim Al-Jafari is elected prime minister of Iraq. Nine weeks later, PUK leader Jalal Talabani is voted president. After reviewing the draft of the new constitution, the Iraqi Turkmen Front presents its list of concerns on its content and its lack of rights for minorites. On October 15, a referendum on the constitution is held and the ITF votes "No" to its present wording. Despite concerns expressed by many groups, the constitution is accepted. On December 15, a parliamentary election is held. MARAM, an organization with representation from many parties, is formed to reject the electoral results, stating that irregularities in voting procedures and fraud raise doubt as to the results.

– *This information is drawn from files from the book* Among the 'Others': Encounters with the Forgotten Turkmen of Iraq, *published in 2004 by Esprit de Corps Books.*

INDEX

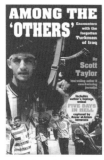